ARTS AND LITERATURE IN ANCIENT MESOPOTAMIA

LUCENT LIBRARY *of* HISTORICAL ERAS

ARTS AND LITERATURE IN ANCIENT MESOPOTAMIA

DON NARDO

LUCENT BOOKS

A part of Gale, Cengage Learning

GALE
CENGAGE Learning

Detroit • New York • San Francisco • New Haven, Conn • Waterville, Maine • London

© 2009 Gale, Cengage Learning

LIBRARY OF CONGRESS CATALOGING-IN-PUBLICATION DATA

Nardo, Don, 1947–
  Arts and literature in ancient Mesopotamia / by Don Nardo.
    p. cm. — (Lucent library of historical eras)
  Includes bibliographical references and index.
  ISBN 978-1-4205-0099-8 (hardcover)
  1. Iraq—Civilization—To 634—Juvenile literature. 2. Middle Eastern literature—History and criticism—Juvenile literature. 3. Arts—Iraq—History—To 1500—Juvenile literature. I. Title.
  DS69.5.N3 2008
  700.935—dc22
                                                                              2008022045

Lucent Books
27500 Drake Rd.
Farmington Hills, MI 48331

ISBN-13: 978-1-4205-0099-8
ISBN-10: 1-4205-0099-6

Printed in the United States of America
2 3 4 5 6 7 13 12 11 10 09

Contents

Foreword

Looking back from the vantage point of the present, history can be viewed as a myriad of intertwining roads paved by human events. Some paths stand out—broad highways whose mileposts, even from a distance of centuries, are clear. The events that propelled the rise to power of Germany's Third Reich, its role in World War II, and its eventual demise, for example, are well defined and documented.

Other roads are less distinct, their route sometimes hidden from view. Modern legislatures may have developed from old tribal councils, for example, but the links between them are indistinct in places, open to discussion and interpretation.

The architecture of civilization—law, religion, art, science, and government—as well as the more everyday aspects of our culture—what we eat, what we wear—all developed along the historical roads and byways. In that progression can be traced every facet of modern life.

A broad look back along these roads reveals that many paths—though of vastly different character—seem to converge at a few critical junctions. These intersections are those great historical eras that echo over the long, steady course of human history, extending beyond the past and into the present.

These epic periods of time are the focus of Historical Eras. They shine through the mists of history like beacons, illuminated by a burst of creativity that propels events forward—so bright that we, from thousands of years away, can clearly see the chain of events leading to the present.

Each Historical Eras consists of a set of books that highlight various aspects of these major eras. For example, the Elizabethan England library features volumes on Queen Elizabeth I and her court, Elizabethan theater, the great playwrights, and everyday life in Elizabethan London.

The mini-library approach allows for the division of each era into its most significant and most interesting parts and the exploration of those parts in depth. Also, social and cultural trends as well as illustrative documents and eyewitness accounts can be prominently featured in individual volumes.

Historical Eras presents a wealth of information to young readers. The lively narrative, fully documented primary and secondary source quotations, maps, photographs, sidebars, and annotated bibliographies serve as launching points for class discussion and further research.

In studying the great historical eras, students also develop a better understanding of our own times. What we learn from the past and how we apply it in the present may shape the future and may determine whether our era will be a guiding light to those traveling future roads.

Introduction

TINY REMAINS OF VAST CULTURAL WEALTH

In ancient times, the region now called Mesopotamia (meaning "the land between the rivers") encompassed what is now Iraq and small portions of neighboring regions. It was here that the world's first cities rose from the then fertile plains of the Tigris-Euphrates river valley. In those cities, human beings first invented systems of writing and created works of literature. The early Mesopotamians were also the first to organize industries and shops run by merchants, craft workers, and artisans.

These pioneering examples of literature and arts and crafts strongly influenced those produced in later places and times. Indeed, at least some of the cultural roots for many later civilizations, including those of Greece, Rome, and later European lands, lie embedded in the ruins of ancient Mesopotamia. "Their towers and temples," University of Windsor scholar Stephen Bertman points out, along with their "farmers, merchants, and artisans who lived out their daily lives; [their] scribes who told their story in the world's oldest writing; and [their] works of literature that still survive, [all] speak of a search for meaning in a land that so often saw the hopes of humankind frustrated [by] nature's raw power or man's voracious greed."[1]

Much Remains Unknown

Bertman's use of the phrase "that still survive" is crucial in examining and understanding ancient Mesopotamia's mighty cultural legacy to later civilizations. Many of the surviving sculptures, paintings, pottery, and epic poems created by its peoples—Sumerians, Babylonians, Assyrians, and Persians, among numerous others—are unarguably impressive. Yet both in diversity and quantity, they only scratch the surface, so to speak. The amount of artistic and literary antiquities (ancient artifacts) these peoples actually produced over the course of dozens of centuries was truly enormous. But most of this tremendous cultural output did not survive the ravages of time and human folly. As the late, great archaeologist of Mesopotamian cities, Seton Lloyd, put it:

> The total of existing antiquities [from ancient Mesopotamia] is no more than a chance residue—microscopically small—of the vast wealth accumulated in their time by the ancient peoples [of the region].

From the same modest total of remains, supplemented by equally small relics of their literature, the daily lives, mental processes, and general behavior . . . of these peoples have been reconstructed with astonishing ingenuity [by] modern scholars. [Yet] there is still a great deal about these ancient peoples that we do not know.[2]

Moreover, archaeologists and other modern experts who try to piece together a recognizable picture of ancient Mesopotamian culture have encountered another challenge. Namely, what

The region that is now referred to as Mesopotamia originally encompassed what is now Iraq and small portions of neighboring regions.

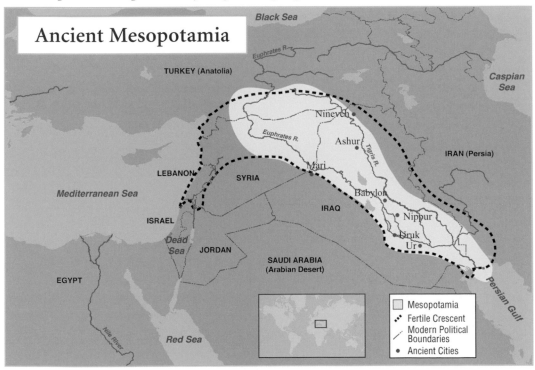

The quest to learn more about life in ancient Mesopotamia continues today with excavations of sites such as this one discovered near Mosul, Iraq, in 2001, at which workers clean a statue of a winged bull dated to the eighth century B.C.

little physical evidence *has* survived is unevenly distributed, both in place and time. For instance, excavators have found a fair amount of sculptures and other artifacts produced by the war-like Assyrians in their period of greatest imperial expansion (the first few centuries of the first millennium B.C.). And numerous poems and other literary works written in the third millennium B.C. by the region's first city builders, the Sumerians, have survived. But sadly, these and a few other similar examples are exceptions to the rule. The surviving historical and cultural evidence for many other ancient Mesopotamian peoples, regions, and eras is very limited. And even considerable periods and aspects of the Sumerian and Assyrian civilizations remain sketchy or even blank. "By sheer coincidence," German scholar Wolfram von Soden writes,

> we are dependent in many areas upon sometimes very extensive, sometimes lesser, or sometimes nonexistent finds. Consequently, a [complete and comprehensive] presentation of the history and cultures [of ancient Mesopotamia] is and will long remain impossible. [The reliability of that presentation] will always be determined in part by the respective availability or lack of [surviving] material. We will do well if we always remain aware of that fact.[3]

Back into the Dust

Thus, the following survey of ancient Mesopotamian arts, crafts, writing systems, and literature is in large degree limited by random factors. Some archaeologists have been fortunate enough to dig in the right places at the right times. And what they have unearthed has greatly enriched humanity's knowledge of some of its earliest civilized endeavors. But much remains buried beneath the streets of modern cities or unknown parts of the windswept plains. And surely much more has been purposely destroyed or else decayed and crumbled back into the dust making up those ancient plains. Considering these realities, people today must count themselves lucky that some remnants of the region's once vast cultural wealth do still exist. They stand, in mute testimony, to the remarkable achievements of a group of peoples who, as one scholar says, constituted one of the "major formative elements for all subsequent civilization."[4]

Chapter One

CRAFTS AND CRAFT WORKERS

The first physical aspects of human civilization—well before towns, cities, and nations arose—were handmade crafts. In the Near East, now called the Middle East, several kinds of craft work were already fairly highly developed when agriculture first appeared in around 9000 B.C. That great watershed in the human saga occurred in what modern experts call the Fertile Crescent. It stretched in a great arc along Mesopotamia's western and northern rim, from Palestine and Syria (along the Mediterranean coast), through what are now Armenia, northern Iraq, and northwestern Iran. People from this well-watered, mostly forested region began migrating eastward or southward onto the Mesopotamian plains between 6000 and 5000 B.C. (between seven thousand and eight thousand years ago). Archaeological evidence shows that by 5000 B.C., these early Mesopotamians were making

pottery, leather clothes, interwoven reed baskets, stone figurines, and other artifacts requiring specialized skills.

These special craft skills became so important in Mesopotamian society that people coined a word to describe a person who became skilled in them. This word, literally translated as "specialist," was *ummia*. Later, the Sumerians, who began building the world's first cities in southern Mesopotamia in the late fourth millennium (the late 3000s) B.C., adopted this word. And not long afterward, the Akkadians began using a similar word to describe craft workers, artisans, and other specialists—*ummanu*. (*Akkadian* is a term modern scholars use to describe the early inhabitants of northern Mesopotamia.)

The rise of urban centers and city life stimulated widespread trade, a class of merchants and traders, and shops to supply a growing range of products demanded by the residents of the cities (and the villages lying on the outskirts of each city). These products had to be made, of course. And by the mid-second millennium B.C., all cities and towns in Sumer and elsewhere in the Near East had a subclass of craft workers. Among others, they included potters, brick makers, carpenters, metalworkers (specialists in copper, bronze, iron, silver, and gold), glassmakers, leatherworkers, weavers and basket makers, jewelers, and wagon makers. These and other craft workers and artisans remained absolutely essential to the economies and social life of the ancient peoples who followed in Mesopotamia, including the Babylonians, Assyrians, and Persians.

Learning a Craft

Within the social structures of those peoples, craft workers belonged mostly to the lower classes (although a few were middle class). The main reason that most craft workers were not well-to-do was that they made things individually, by hand. This was time consuming. So a person could produce only a few items of average or high quality in a day. And he or she usually made very little profit from any single item. Nevertheless, evidence suggests that a skilled craft worker could make a decent enough living to own a modest house and raise a family.

In fact, family played an important role in the lives and professions of ancient Mesopotamian craft workers. Many workers passed knowledge of their professions down to their sons, nephews, grandsons, daughters, or other younger relatives. At their own discretion, they might also teach their skills to the offspring of fellow

Where Did the Tin Come From?

Scholars are still somewhat unsure about the exact sources for the tin the ancient Mesopotamians used to make bronze. No tin existed in Mesopotamia itself. Gwendolyn Leick, a leading expert on the ancient Near East, speculates:

No cuneiform sources reveal the place of origin of tin, only its sites of distribution. It is likely that tin was mined in eastern Anatolia [what is now Turkey] during the third millennium [B.C.], however, Assyrian merchants brought tin to Anatolia, where it was traded for locally produced silver. It has been suggested that at that time tin came from much farther east, from Afghanistan, perhaps because Anatolian mines had been exhausted. . . . In the later second and in the first millennium [B.C.], eastern Anatolia once again supplied tin, as Hittite and Assyrian sources seem to indicate.

Gwendolyn Leick, *Historical Dictionary of Mesopotamia.* Lanham, MD: Scarecrow, 2003, p. 119.

workers, friends, or other people in the community.

There were no universities or schools for these workers. So knowledge of a craft was passed from one generation to the next through the apprentice system. If the apprentice worked hard and gained enough knowledge and skill, he or she became a journeyman, or competent (though average) worker. And in time the person might become a master, or expert, craft worker who could take in a number of his or her own young and unskilled apprentices. According to Von Soden:

> The apprentices working under the journeyman readily called him, as their comrade, the "big brother." The apprentices concluded a contract . . . with the master [craft worker], who demanded a complete apprenticeship from them and set down the necessary payment. . . . Since the knowledge of a craft was not fixed in writing, such knowledge could only be mediated by means of an intensive oral and practical apprenticeship.[5]

The relationship between the master and the apprentice, who often lived in the master's house for several years, could become quite close, even like father and son. Consequently, laws developed to protect the master, as well as the apprentice's own parents. Among the statutes in the famous law code of the Babylonian king Hammurabi (reigned ca. 1792–1750 B.C.) was one that reads: "If a [master craft worker] has undertaken to rear a child and teaches him his craft, he [the apprentice] can not be demanded back [by the apprentice's parents]." In such a case, the apprentice was, for all intents and purposes, the master's foster or adopted child. In contrast, another of Hammurabi's laws states: "If he [the master] has not taught him [the apprentice] his craft, this adopted son may return to his father's house."[6]

Close social ties also frequently developed among most or all of the workers within a single profession in a city. And it was common for them to band together into a guild. Such guilds were not modern-style unions that organized strikes in order to get higher pay or achieve political goals. Rather, an ancient Mesopotamian craft guild was more of a fellowship of individuals who shared certain skills and lifestyles. Members met socially outside of work and perhaps traveled and worshipped together. Each guild had to register with an administrator in the local royal palace. Guilds could not become independent of the city's authorities, mainly because of the difficulty in getting many of the raw materials necessary to the craft workers' trades. In particular, the Mesopotamian plains had very limited supplies of metals, stone, and wood (because there were few forests). And for the most part, the governments of the city-states paid for and oversaw the business negotiations for these raw materials from neighboring regions.

"The Archaeologist's Best Friend"

In contrast, one raw material that Mesopotamia had in abundance was clay for making ceramic, or pottery, objects. This was important because jars, bowls, cups, figurines, and other ceramic items were the most common products made by Mesopotamian craft workers. In short, nearly everyone used pottery objects on a daily basis. Moreover, these objects have turned out to be no less important to modern investigators of ancient Mesopotamian civilization. As one expert puts it, "Pottery is the archaeologist's best friend."[7] The reason is that these items were breakable and constantly being replaced over the course of centuries and

Pottery jars and other items made of clay are plentiful among the ruins of ancient Mesopotamia. Their varying styles through the centuries allow archaeologists to accurately date the buildings in which such pieces are found as well as other items found nearby.

millennia. Because the styles of ceramic objects changed on a regular basis, the replacement items were often distinct from the originals. The various pottery styles in the region have been dated with some confidence. So the remains of ancient pottery can be used to date the buildings in which they are found and/or the cultural remains found beside them. Crude ceramic objects existed in the Near East as early as 7000 B.C. At first, such objects were shaped by hand and baked for random periods in open fires. Eventually, however, kilns, which gave the potter considerably more control over the process, came into use. University of Wales scholar H.W.F. Saggs speculates about how early potters in the region learned these basics over time:

> One can imagine people using [crude clay pots] for cooking food over an open fire, and, on subsequently finding that [the pots] had become hard and waterproof, recognizing their usefulness. Early production [of ceramic items] must have been hit-or-miss. [But] a time must have come when someone must have thought of enclosing the clay vessels for baking in a container fixed above a fire pit, to give better management of the process. One can see how such a system could eventually develop into a kiln, in which the potters had close control over the burning conditions and could achieve very high temperatures.[8]

Even after the introduction of kilns, potters continued to hand shape their products, or else they pressed the moist clay into simple molds they had carved in the desired shapes. A major step forward occurred with the introduction of a slow-turning, hand-operated potter's wheel in Mesopotamia circa 4000 B.C. This made possible small-scale mass production of vases, bowls, and other ceramic items, which helped meet the demands of growing local populations. In around 2000 B.C., a wheel that turned even faster came into use. This allowed potters to make vessels with very thin walls, as well as delicate spouts, handles, and covers. Still another innovation—coating ceramic objects with colored glazes—was introduced by Assyrian and Babylonian potters in the early first millennium B.C.

Metalworkers and Their Craft

Unlike potters, Mesopotamian metalworkers (or metalsmiths, or more simply, smiths) had to rely mostly on imported supplies of raw materials. Their copper, for instance, came mainly from Iran, Anatolia (what is now Turkey), and Palestine. The first metal to be widely used in the ancient Near East, copper, was smelted (melted down) and cast into tools, eating utensils, weapons, jewelry, and numerous other products. Copper was also the main ingredient in another pivotal metal used in the region—bronze. According to noted scholar Gwendolyn Leick, bronze began

Copper, the first metal to be widely used in the Near East and the main ingredient in bronze, was used by metalworkers to create a variety of practical and decorative products, including this nail and support depicting King Ur-Nanshe of Lagash, dated from 2800 B.C.

to be used in large quantities in Mesopotamia around 3000 B.C.

[It] was first produced as an alloy [mixture] of copper and antimony or lead, [and] later as an alloy of copper and tin. It was either made by smelting a mixture of copper ores and tin ores, or by melting together metallic copper and tin. Their ratio varied from 6:1 [6 parts copper to 1 part tin] to 10:1, depending on the function of the objects [made from the bronze].[9]

Other metals were used for both practical and decorative objects in ancient Mesopotamia, though in considerably smaller quantities than copper and bronze. These included brass (an alloy of copper and zinc), gold, silver, and electrum (a mixture of gold and silver). The smelting of iron, which is harder and more durable than the metals mentioned above, did not begin in Mesopotamia until roughly 1200 B.C. (This industry was pioneered by the Hittites, who created a powerful kingdom in the heart of Anatolia in the second millennium B.C.)

To smelt these metals, Mesopotamian smiths placed the ores containing the metals, along with smaller amounts of charcoal, in stone-lined furnaces similar to but larger than kilns. The heat produced by the furnaces caused the flecks of pure metal imbedded in the ore to separate out. After the copper or other metal had been smelted, the smith cast it into cups, bowls, figurines, and/or numerous other metal artifacts. Samuel N. Kramer, one of the twentieth century's leading archaeologists of ancient Mesopotamia, describes the most common casting methods:

> The molten metal was cast into either flat, open molds or three-dimensional closed molds. Some richly decorated castings were even produced by the complicated "lost wax" method, in which the original matrix [the item's shape] was modeled in wax, then coated with clay. [Next] the wax was melted away to leave its design in the inner surface of the clay.[10]

The smith then poured liquid metal into the hollow clay mold he or she had created. And when the metal had solidified, the smith removed the clay, revealing the finished metal item.

The smelting and molding process was more difficult for iron than for copper, bronze, and other metals. This is because working with iron requires higher temperatures. In fact, none of the furnaces used in ancient times could produce temperatures as high as iron's melting point (about 2,800 degrees F, or about 1,538 degrees C). So the smiths resorted to a process known as forging. They heated the iron until it turned into a spongy mass containing carbon and other impurities. Then when the metal was still hot, they hammered it, which shaped it and removed some of the impurities. The neo-Assyrians used iron swords and other weapons made this way to great effect; iron-forging was a contributing factor in their creation of a vast empire in the early first millennium B.C.

Jewelry and Carved Ivory

Another important group of craft workers in ancient Mesopotamia, jewelers, also relied on imported raw materials. This is because both precious metals (gold and silver) and semiprecious stones (agate, lapis lazuli, jasper, crystal, and others) were in short supply in the Tigris-Euphrates valley. Anatolia and northern Iran were the main sources of gold and silver. And lapis lazuli, a stone having an intense and striking blue color, was mined mainly in what is now Afghanistan. (The manufacture of jewelry in Mesopotamia from these imported supplies of metals and stones was not the only source of the jewelry worn in the region. During military campaigns into

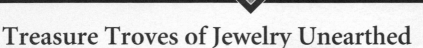

Treasure Troves of Jewelry Unearthed

Some of the finest examples of ancient Mesopotamian jewelry were unearthed by the renowned British archaeologist Charles Leonard Woolley in the royal cemetery at Ur. Between 1926 and 1932, he excavated sixteen tombs dating from the early to mid-third millennium B.C. Of the numerous jewelry items these tombs yielded, those belonging to Queen Puabi (in Sumerian, Queen Shubad), who lived sometime between 2600 and 2500 B.C., are particularly stunning. These include gold and silver pins for fastening clothes; a crown made of gold and lapis lazuli; and necklaces of gold, silver, and lapis lazuli. Another notable collection of ancient Mesopotamian jewelry was discovered in 1988 by Iraqi archaeologist Mazahim Mahmud Hussein in the remains of the Assyrian city of Nimrud. Three of the city's royal tombs contained more than fifteen hundred jewelry items. Among them is a royal crown decorated with eight winged girls and a dome of gold leaves.

Jewelry from the tomb of Queen Puabi, including pins, necklaces, earrings, and hair ornaments, are among the finds of British archaeologist Charles Leonard Woolley.

foreign lands, particularly those of the neo-Assyrian monarchs, soldiers seized large quantities of ready-made jewelry as booty and brought it home.)

The finely made jewelry items produced by Mesopotamian jewelers were routinely worn by both men and women. Beginning in the early third millennium B.C., men often wore both bracelets and strings of beads. Later, in the first millennium B.C., Assyrian men and women donned various sorts of jewelry, including bracelets and earrings crafted into rings, cones, and crescent shapes. People also used jewelry to decorate statues of gods and as wedding gifts.

A necklace discovered in the royal cemetery of Ur, dated 2600 B.C. and strung with beads of gold, lapis lazuli, and carnelian, is an example of the intricate work of ancient Mesopotamian jewelry makers.

To make earrings and other jewelry items from gold, silver, or other metals, jewelers first cut thin sheets of metal into small pieces. Then they used hammers, bronze tweezers, grinding stones, and other tools to shape the pieces. A jar containing such tools was found in the ruins of the Sumerian (and later Babylonian) city of Larsa. These tools belonged to a craft worker named Ilsu-Ibnisu, one of only a handful of ancient Mesopotamian jewelers whose names have survived.

Ivory was another rare and precious material used by ancient Mesopotamian craft workers. It came mostly from the tusks of elephants, which existed in parts of the Near East until they were hunted to extinction in the first millennium B.C. Ivory was also imported from India after around 2000 B.C. Although carved ivory was made into jewelry in Mesopotamia, it had a wide range of other ornamental uses. Yale University scholar Karen R. Nemet-Nejat lists the major ones:

Ivory was used to make small objects, such as boxes, handles, spoons, and combs. Ivory plaques were carved in relief [and] often dyed, inlaid with other materials, or overlaid with gold leaf, and then inserted into or joined with parts of wooden furniture for

Craft workers in ancient Mesopotamia used ivory to create jewelry, small decorative objects, and ornamental carvings such as this plaque dated from the eighth to seventh centuries B.C.

decoration. Many of the subjects depicted [in stone carvings] on the walls of Assyrian palaces were repeated on the [smaller] ivory carvings of the period, such as battle scenes, divine animals, [and] gods.[11]

Glassmaking

Still another craft that produced items highly prized across ancient Mesopotamia (and the rest of the Near East) was glassmaking. Evidence indicates that it began sometime in the third millennium

Before the advent of glassblowing, glassmakers used several different methods to make glass items. The methods included the "open mold" method, the "core-forming" method, the "lost wax" method, and the "cold-cutting" method. Shown here is a fluted glass bottle from the Kassite dynasty in Ur, dated from 1500 to 1200 B.C.

Mesopotamian Mapmaking

One ancient Mesopotamian craft often overlooked in modern studies is mapmaking (cartography). Maps created in ancient Mesopotamia were drawn, like modern versions, as if seen from above. Mostly they were carved into clay tablets, and because it was tricky to etch curved lines in the wet clay, most lines in the maps were straight, even when showing a road or boundary that actually curved. Many of these maps were made to show the boundaries of farms and estates, the ground plans of temples and houses, and the layout of cities. There was even a map, dating from around 600 B.C., depicting the world as a whole. Now called the *mappa mundi*, it shows the earth as a round disk surrounded by a double ring of ocean. Babylon lies at the center of the disk. This and other ancient Mesopotamian maps were not drawn to scale. (An exception is a highly accurate map of the city of Nippur dating to the second millennium B.C.) Canals were sometimes drawn as parallel lines with wavy crests between them to specify water. And little

An example of ancient Mesopotamian mapmaking dating from around 600 B.C. depicts Babylon at the center of the earth, surrounded by rings that represent the ocean.

rectangles or circles marked cities and towns. There were also lines for streets and roads, in many cases including street names.

B.C. However, no glass objects from this period have survived. The earliest surviving Mesopotamian glass products date from around 1600 B.C. After that, glass objects became more and more common in the region (although the craft temporarily declined between 1200 and 800 B.C. due to trade disruptions caused by war, folk migrations, and other factors). Still, glass items were for a long time fairly expensive. So most members of the lower classes could not afford them until the first century B.C. At that time, a glass-maker in Syria introduced the technique of glassblowing, which made glassmaking faster and easier and glass products much cheaper to buy.

Before the advent of glassblowing, glassmakers used several methods to make items such as perfume bottles; vases; beads for earrings, pendants, and other jewelry; figurines; and the pupils of the eyes of stone statues. The method used depended on whether the finished object would be solid or hollow. "For solid objects" such as "beads, pendants, amulets, and figurines," Stephen Bertman explains,

> the "open mold" method was used. Molten glass was simply poured into molds and, when cooled, took on their shape. . . . For hollow objects like vases and bottles, a different method was used, called "core-forming." A core was modeled out of mud mixed with straw or clay mixed with manure. A rod was then stuck into the top of the mass. Next, the artisan—holding the rod—dipped the core into molten glass. . . . After the vessel was totally cool, the rod would be removed and the core broken up and shaken out, leaving a hollow vessel.[12]

In addition, early glassmakers sometimes used the same lost wax method employed by metalsmiths; the difference was that molten glass, rather than molten metal, was poured into the three-dimensional molds. A fourth method, called cold cutting, began with a sizable lump of molten glass. The glassmaker carefully cut off pieces of it and then molded each piece into the shape desired and allowed it to cool.

The results of these methods were often stunning. Using a blend of collected knowledge passed from generation to generation, ingenuity, and sheer hard work and patience, ancient Mesopotamian glassmakers left their mark on history. Like many other craft workers of that long-ago time and place, they produced numerous items that were no less beautiful and useful than the finest ones made today.

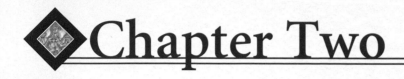

Chapter Two

SCULPTURE AND OTHER FINE ARTS

The peoples of ancient Mesopotamia did not, as most people do today, recognize sculpture, painting, and music as so-called fine arts. For example, a Mesopotamian who painted images on walls, sculpted statues, or fashioned mosaics was not seen as somehow separate from and more lofty than a metalsmith, jeweler, or potter. Rather, he or she was just another specialist, or craft worker. And a musician was not even that. Society viewed someone who could play an instrument and perhaps compose tunes not as an inspired artist but simply as a person with a useful skill. Thus, though it is easier for modern readers to examine what they see as crafts and arts separately, it must be kept in mind that the ancient Mesopotamians did not make such distinctions.

As for the artists themselves, almost nothing is known. Like other craft workers, they belonged mostly to the lower classes. And the vast majority of the region's surviving writings describe only the lives and achievements of the wealthy and noble. As the late, great scholar of ancient Mesopotamia A. Leo Oppenheim put it: "References to artists and their work are rare even in [ancient Mesopotamian] letters. [Modern scholars have been able to] gather some data concerning works of art and their manufacture . . . from royal inscriptions, [but] the personalities of the artists [themselves] remain completely beyond our reach."[13]

Early Mesopotamian Sculptures

Among the greatest accomplishments of these now anonymous artisans were large numbers of magnificent sculptures. Most of the major ancient Mesopotamian peoples—from the Sumerians and

Babylonians to the Persians—created magnificent examples. However, modern experts have singled out the sculpted works produced by the Assyrians during their last period of imperial expansion (the early first millennium B.C.) as particularly impressive.

There were two main forms of Assyrian and other ancient Mesopotamian sculpture. One consisted of freestanding, three-dimensional statues, mostly depicting kings, gods, and mythical beings. The other was reliefs (or bas-reliefs), carved scenes raised somewhat from flat surfaces, usually walls, though reliefs were also carved on doors, furniture, vases, pillars, and other objects.

The earliest high-quality sculptures in Mesopotamia were produced by the Sumerians. Some were carved from wood. Others featured wooden cores covered with metal, and still others were of stone, most often alabaster, limestone, and gypsum. Of the Sumerian stone sculptures, some fine examples belong to a set of twelve gypsum and alabaster figurines dating from roughly 2700 B.C. They were discovered in A.D. 1932 at Eshnunna (modern-day Tell Asmar), situated about 50 miles (80km) northeast of modern Baghdad, Iraq. These statuettes are striking for the oversize eyes the sculptors gave their subjects, who seem to be worshippers bearing gifts for a god or gods.

Another set of beautifully made Sumerian statues was found in the ruins of Lagash, located some 120 miles (193km) northwest of modern Basra, Iraq. Num-

bering close to thirty, these carved figures, which vary in size, depict one of the city's great rulers, King Gudea. Reigning from circa 2141 to 2122 B.C., he made a mark as a patron of arts and architecture,

Excavation of the ruins of Lagash revealed several sculptures depicting King Gudea, the Sumerian leader who ensured that history would remember him by commissioning these monuments to himself, nearly thirty of which have been discovered.

King Sargon's Stone Guardian in Chicago

Among the more impressive sculptures produced by the ancient Assyrians were the huge human-headed bulls that guarded their royal palaces. A spokesperson for the University of Chicago's famed Oriental Institute describes the giant bull-man on display there:

Part bull, part bird, part man, a massive stone sculpture that once stood guard in the throne room of the royal palace in Dur-Sharrukin now impresses visitors to the University of Chicago's Oriental Institute Museum.

Standing 16 feet tall, the massive stone sculpture presides over the west end of the gallery. [It] represents a *lamassu*, or guardian figure, and has the body of a bull, the wings of a bird, and the head of a man. He wears a horned crown, which in ancient Mesopotamia was reserved for divine figures. The bull was part of a royal palace in ancient Dur-Sharrukin (Fortress of Sargon), a new capital city founded by the Assyrian king Sargon II shortly after he came to the throne in 721 B.C. Oriental Institute archaeologists discovered the sculpture in 1929, during excavation of the palace in northern Iraq, on the site which is known today as Khorsabad. The bull weighs an estimated 40 tons and was a difficult object to move both in antiquity and in modern times. In ancient times, crews of men used ropes and levers to remove the monolith from a quarry and drag it to Dur-Sharrukin.

Quoted in Oriental Institute at the University of Chicago, "Assyrian Bull Provides Museum Focal Point." http://news.uchicago.edu/releases/03/oi/030630.oi-bull.shtml.

erecting more than a dozen religious temples. Gudea wanted to make sure that future generations knew who built these structures. So he ordered the carving of the statues as timeless monuments to himself. (To this end, he was successful, since these sculptures have survived for over four thousand years!)

Thanks to the talents of ancient sculptors, we know what another famous early Mesopotamian ruler looked like. He was the Akkadian empire-builder Sargon of

Akkad, who reigned from around 2340 to 2284 B.C. In this case, the artisan first fashioned a detailed bust of the king, probably using wax. Then, the lost wax method was used to transform it into the magnificent bronze head that now rests in a museum in Baghdad.

A carving of a bull's head adorned with gold leaf and lapis lazuli was discovered in the tomb of Sumerian queen Puabi and is shown attached to a reconstruction of a wooden lyre to depict the work's completed form as it was originally crafted around 2600 B.C.

In addition to fine statues, figurines, and busts, Sumerian and Akkadian sculptors carved many splendid decorative and ornamental versions of animals. Among the most dramatic examples is a surviving high relief from the Sumerian city of Al-Ubaid, not far from Ur. (A high relief is a relief in which the figures remain attached to a flat background but are carved almost fully in three dimensions.) Dating from 3000 B.C. or perhaps earlier, the large-scale work measures more than 3 feet (1m) high and more than 8 feet (2.4m) wide. It shows Imdugud, a lion-headed eagle from Sumerian mythology, with its wings spread wide; beneath the wings stand two large stags, each with a huge set of antlers. Another splendid ornament carved by Sumerian artisans was found in nearby Ur. It consists of a bull's head attached to the sound box of a lyre (small harp). The object was first carved from wood and then covered by gold leaf and lapis lazuli.

Assyrian and Persian Sculpture

Bulls were also frequently depicted in Assyrian sculpture. The largest and most visually arresting examples are several surviving human-headed bulls that originally guarded the entrances to the Assyrian palaces. They were called both *lamassi*, meaning "bull-men," and *aladlammu*, meaning "protective spirits." Each of these immense pieces, weighing up to 20 tons (18t), has a beard and wings.

Even more famous are the long panels of relief sculptures that once adorned the

Sculpture That Tells a Story

The sculpted battle reliefs adorning the walls of Assyrian palaces are among the finest surviving examples of ancient Near Eastern art. The noted twentieth-century archaeologist and scholar Seton Lloyd tells the story that unfolds in one such relief:

The Assyrian army prepares for war. Led by the king, it crosses difficult country on the way to attack a walled city. . . . The city is taken, burned, and demolished. The enemy leaders are punished with ingenious brutality. A victory is then celebrated. In the inscriptions [accompanying the carved figures], the outcome of a minor campaign of this sort is recorded by the laconic comment, "So I came upon them and destroyed them utterly and turned their cities into forgotten mounds." . . . The scenes themselves are often arranged episodically—that is, they represent successive developments in the progress of a single action—and if one examines them in detail, one sees that at no time is the overall outcome anticipated. The king himself in his chariot is in obvious danger from enemy archers, from whom at times he appears most inadequately protected. [But, of course, he always emerges unhurt and victorious.]

Seton Lloyd, *The Art of the Ancient Near East.* London: Thames and Hudson, 1965, pp. 197–98.

---

walls of the palaces erected by the neo-Assyrian kings. Made of gypsum, they show military battles, large-scale building projects, and other notable achievements of these monarchs. On the one hand, these reliefs were propaganda designed to impress both Assyrian subjects and foreign visitors. On the other, they were decorative art of extremely high quality. Indeed, "from the artistic point of view," in the words of noted historian Chester G. Starr,

Assyrian relief was the highest point thus far reached in Near Eastern art. Sieges and battles at times had almost a sense of space, and in the scenes of hunting, animals were shown with more realism than had ever before been achieved. Here the artists gave a vivid sense of motion, even at times of pity for the dying lions or wild asses. In other scenes the king, with fringed robe, long curled beard, and heavy shoulders and legs, was a static but powerful figure.[14]

Though clearly gifted artists, the sculptors who carved these massive panels of reliefs had not yet learned the principle of showing true perspective. That is, they

A scene from the alabaster relief found in the ruins of the palace of King Ashurbanipal depicts the Assyrian leader bravely slaying a lion, one of the many feats portrayed among the panels that once adorned the palace walls.

did not make increasingly distant human figures and other carved objects look progressively smaller than nearer ones. To suggest that one object lay behind another, they instead placed the more distant one above the nearer one. Still, even with this limitation, the neo-Assyrian battle reliefs are often breathtaking in their levels of realism and detail.

In fact, these reliefs were so impressive that they strongly influenced later Mesopotamian sculptors. In particular, Persian artisans borrowed a number of artistic styles and themes from Assyrian art. Many Persian sculptures also dem-

onstrate heavy Greek influences, in large part because many of the sculptors who worked on Persian temples and palaces came from Persian-controlled Greek cities in western Anatolia. These Greek artisans excelled at giving carved human figures a quality of depth, such as showing realistic anatomical features beneath the figures' clothes.

Perhaps the most impressive of the ancient Persian reliefs were those carved on the Behistun Rock, a sheer-sided peak situated not far east of Babylon. Commissioned by one of Persia's greatest monarchs, King Darius I (reigned ca.

522–486 B.C.), it shows him lording over ten of his enemies. Nine are tied by ropes, while the tenth lies sprawled under his feet. Later, the Sassanians, who prided themselves on reviving Persian religion and art, created very similar cliff carvings. Some show royal hunting scenes; others depict Sassanian rulers battling their archenemies, the Romans.

Both freestanding statues and carved reliefs fashioned by Sumerian, Assyrian, Persian, and other Mesopotamian sculptors did not have plain, colorless surfaces, as most surviving examples do today. Rather, these works were originally painted, usually in bright colors. In most cases, the paints disintegrated over the centuries, although a few traces of the original pigments have survived. They provide evidence that human hair and beards were painted black, carved representations of jewelry were painted yellow, and trees and plants were painted green.

Paintings on Walls and Bricks

Ancient Mesopotamian artisans also painted fine murals on walls and other surfaces inside temples, palaces, and the houses of well-to-do persons. Several of these murals have survived in varying states of preservation. Some of the most impressive examples are those unearthed in Mari (modern-day Tell al-Hariri), an ancient city situated near a bend in the upper Euphrates River. There, in the remnants of the palace of King Zimri-Lim (ca. 1775–1761 B.C.), archaeologists

The Behistun Rock, a relief carved around the fifth century B.C. into a cliffside east of Babylon in what is now Iran, depicts Persian king Darius I dominating ten "imposter king" enemies.

found dozens of wall murals, a number of them in surprisingly good condition. One depicts Zimri-Lim reciting an oath before Ishtar (or Inanna), divine protector of kings (as well as goddess of love and passion). Around these central figures, the painters placed images of other gods and several griffins, mythical creatures that symbolized divine and kingly power.

A section of a mural from the palace of King Tiglathpileser III from the eighth century B.C. depicts the head of a man with a beard and contains remnants of red and black paint.

Other well-preserved wall paintings were discovered in a palace built by the neo-Assyrian monarch Tiglathpileser III (ca. 744–727 B.C.) at Til Barsip, also on the upper Euphrates. Stephen Bertman describes these imposing murals:

[They] show scenes of warfare and hunting. Prisoners of war tied to chariots are escorted to execution by armed soldiers. One Assyrian soldier leads an enemy prisoner by the beard. In a mural over 70 feet long, Tiglathpileser is shown enthroned in majesty, surrounded by members of his army and administrative staff. Elsewhere in the palace, in a bathroom of all places, we see a lion hunt indicative of the Assyrian fascination with power and domination.[15]

To create such a mural, an early Mesopotamian painter first covered the wall's surface with a kind of plaster made by mixing mud and either lime or gypsum. When the plaster was dry, he or she used a pointed tool to sketch the outlines of the picture. In the final step, the paint was applied. Although this dry-surface method continued to be used here and there for centuries afterward, in the late second millennium B.C., the fresco technique became more common across Mesopotamia. A fresco is a painting done on wet plaster. One major benefit of this approach is that the paint and plaster dry together, in the process merging and thereby causing the colors to last longer. A drawback is that the painter is forced to work as fast as possible in order to finish applying the paint before the plaster dries.

As for the paints themselves, the pigments came mostly from mineral substances. Red pigment was made from iron oxide (more commonly called rust), for example. Black paint came from soot or tar; blue from copper oxide or lapis lazuli; green from malachite (a green material resulting from the weathering of copper ores); and white from gypsum. The painter combined these pigments with egg yolks or milk solids, which made them stick better to the wall or one of several other painting surfaces.

Of these other surfaces, one of the more common, especially among the Babylonians and Persians, was decorative bricks. These were placed in noticeable positions on the exteriors of palaces, city gates, and other public structures. The bricks were enameled so that they became highly resistant to the destructive effects of sunlight, wind, and rain. To produce the enamel, the painter mixed pigments with stone dust, which made a glaze he or she then applied directly to the bricks. One of the finest surviving examples is a brightly colored brick painting of a row of Persian archers. It was found in the ruins of the palace of Persia's King Artaxerxes III (358–338 B.C.) at Susa, in western Iran.

Mosaics and Cylinder Seals

Another decorative art applied to walls and other flat surfaces in ancient times was mosaics. A mosaic is a picture made by gluing many small colored stones, tiles, pieces of glass, shells, or other objects to the desired surface. When the Seleucid Greeks controlled Mesopotamia and other sectors of the Near East in the fourth and third centuries B.C., they installed many Greek-style mosaic tile floors in private homes and public buildings. Before this era, mosaics had not been a major art form in Mesopotamia.

However, some mosaics were occasionally created by earlier Mesopotamian peoples. And a few outstanding examples have been found. For example, as early as the fourth millennium B.C., some Ubaidian and Sumerian artisans were practicing a mosaic-like technique that used small, baked clay cones. (*Ubaidian* is the general name modern scholars use to denote the inhabitants of the region before the rise of the Sumerians.) The ends of the cones were dipped in colored pigments or coated with copper. Then the artisans inserted them into cracks in brick walls in such a way that the cones formed simple geometric patterns, including triangles and zigzags.

The most outstanding example of an early Mesopotamian mosaic in a more conventional style is the famous Royal Standard of Ur (or Battle Standard of Ur, or simply Standard of Ur). Probably dating from the third millennium B.C., it was unearthed in A.D. 1927 at Ur by renowned British archaeologist Charles Leonard Woolley. Today, this splendid artifact rests in London's British Museum.

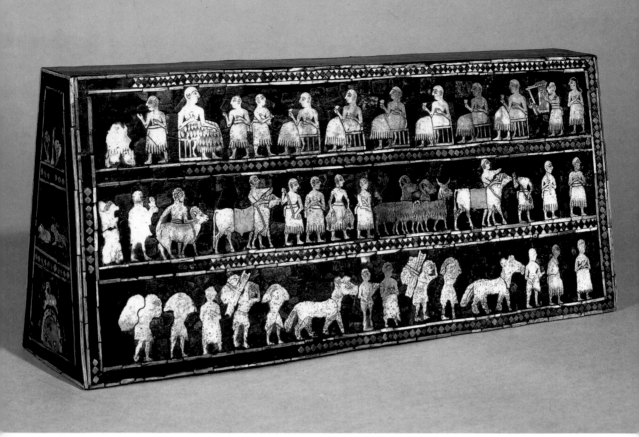

The Standard of Ur, discovered by British archaeologist Charles Leonard Woolley in 1927 in the royal tombs of Ur and dated from the third millennium B.C., depicts a Sumerian military victory within its intricate mosaic design.

The Standard of Ur consists of a wooden box about 8.5 inches (21cm) wide and 19.5 inches (50cm) long covered by tiny pieces of shell, blue lapis lazuli, and red limestone. The mosaic's complex scenes depict a Sumerian military victory and the celebration following it. "The scene shown on one side," in Seton Lloyd's words,

is a battle with chariots and infantry engaged, and on the other [side] a feast is in progress at which a victory is being celebrated, while various forms of booty are paraded before

the participants. In each scene the figure of a king is recognizable by its slightly exaggerated size. As an introduction to the dress, appearance, and behavior of the Sumerians, this is a remarkably revealing document.[16]

Another ancient art form that required the delicate manipulation of tiny materials was the production of cylinder seals. These were small pieces of stone (or at times copper, bronze, gold, ivory, bone, or shell) on which artisans known as seal cutters etched pictures or words. One could press a finished seal into moist clay, rendering a tiny raised image, or stamp. "The purpose of such seals," Gwendolyn Leick explains, "was to indicate the authority of the person or institution who applied the seal impression, rather like a signature on a modern document."[17] Hundreds of thousands, possibly even millions, of cylinder seals were made across ancient Mesopotamia over the centuries.

To make a cylinder seal, a seal cutter used chisels, pointed tools, cutting blades, and hand-turned drills made of copper, bronze, or flint. Using these tools, the seal cutter carved a miniature scene. Such scenes typically showed activities such as feasting, dancing, weaving, cooking, and fighting (often among mythical human heroes).

Musicians and Musical Compositions

Carvings and paintings were not the only products of the more talented and creative inhabitants of ancient Mesopotamia. Archaeological evidence shows that some of them fashioned what today would be called songs. In fact, music played an important role in the religious festivals, royal court gatherings, and communal activities of the Sumerians, Babylonians, and many later peoples in the region. Groups of singers and musicians, both male and female, took part; it is likely that someone in such a group composed some of the tunes performed. (Other songs they performed were probably traditional, dating back several generations.)

Among the songs popular in the Sumerian, Babylonian, and Assyrian periods were odes to various gods and human

Cylinder Seals Provide Useful Information

Ancient Mesopotamian cylinder seals have proved very valuable to archaeologists for two reasons. First, some of the scenes and inscriptions on them reveal facts about Mesopotamian mythology, everyday life, and changing artistic styles. As the late, renowned scholar Samuel N. Kramer put it, "The cylinder seal was in continuous use for 3,000 years, and is found at every archaeological site. It is therefore a record of the habits and activities of kings and common people, and of the changing attitudes toward art and technical craftsmanship." Another reason that cylinder seals are valuable is that they often bear the names of rulers or dates or follow styles distinct to a specific place and time. This allows scholars to give an approximate date for the sites where they are found.

Samuel N. Kramer, *Cradle of Civilization*. New York: Time-Life, 1978, p. 145.

When rolled in clay, this cylinder seal belonging to a Babylonian physician reveals the image of a sphinx. Carved from lapis lazuli, it dates from approximately the sixth century B.C.

rulers, laments for deceased kings, marching music for soldiers, and tunes celebrating weddings, feasts, homecomings, and all manner of communal events. Much later, in Mesopotamia's Seleucid and Parthian periods, Greek-style wandering minstrels sang about famous heroes. Many of these songs, scholar Norman B. Hunt says, "dealt with deeds of valor or referred to myths that were believed to be true." Some were "tales of a rejected lover," others "of a warrior and his enemy."[18]

Ancient Mesopotamian musicians played a wide range of instruments. They included tambourines, small drums, larger drums similar to modern kettle drums, cymbals, small bells, lyres and larger harps, single and double pipes similar to modern flutes or oboes, and clay whistles. Though these instruments were sometimes played solo, at times they were combined into small orchestras.

The players did not make up their parts as they went along. Rather, they followed written scores having the ancient equivalent of modern musical notes. (Babylonian tablets from the second millennium B.C. contain scales of such notes.) Indeed, if a Mesopotamian musician could be suddenly transported to the present day, he or she would likely adapt to playing modern music rather quickly. This, along with the evidence of other ancient Mesopotamian artistry, is revealing. It shows that, despite the passage of thousands of years, artistic talent has remained a constant feature in human civilization.

Chapter Three

LANGUAGE AND WRITING

The invention of writing was one of the chief contributions early Mesopotamian peoples made to the ongoing development of human civilization. Indeed, as Kramer phrases it, this milestone brought about "a revolution in communications that had far-reaching effects on [humanity's] economic, intellectual, and cultural progress."[19] With the ability to write and read, people could now record their financial dealings in detail. They could also communicate over long distances by sending letters and record their medical knowledge, laws, hymns and prayers to the gods, and literature, including epic poems about famous heroes and military leaders.

Mesopotamian Languages

The key to the success of the first writing systems was expressing existing languages as effectively as possible. And one of the great achievements of early Mesopotamian civilization was the introduction of a system that could be adapted to any of these tongues. The first language to achieve widespread use in the region both verbally and in writing was Sumerian. Scholars remain uncertain about its original source. But there is no question that by the close of the fourth millennium B.C., it had largely replaced any older languages in southern Mesopotamia. Of those older tongues, the main one, today called Ubaidian, contributed a number of words (called loan words) to Sumerian. Among others, they include the names of various cities and of the region's major rivers, the Tigris and Euphrates. Once Sumerian was routinely committed to writing, it became the official language of administration and correspondence in Mesopotamia for many centuries.

This situation began to change early in the second millennium B.C., when Sumerian rapidly declined as a spoken language.

(After around 1600 B.C. it continued to be used by scholars in the same way that European priests and scholars continued to use Latin long after it had ceased to be spoken.) Among the languages that replaced Sumerian for everyday use were Semitic tongues that entered Mesopotamia from the west. One, Akkadian, steadily developed into several dialects. The two principal ones were Assyrian and Babylonian (spoken in northern and southern Mesopotamia, respectively). Akkadian had become the chief language of business and correspondence in Mesopotamia by the mid-second millennium B.C.

Several other languages also entered Mesopotamia in the third and second millennia B.C. These included Elamite, spoken primarily in Elam (lying along Mesopotamia's eastern side); Hurrian, used mainly in Mitanni (a kingdom lying west of Assyria); and two important Semitic languages—Aramaic and Amorite. Aramaic eventually became the most widely spoken and written language of the Near East. In the words of H.W.F. Saggs, a leading expert of the ancient languages of the region: "The trading activities of the Aramaeans spread their language over much of the Near East. [Aramaic] had the

Samuel Kramer: Extraordinary Translator

Sumerian was eventually largely deciphered thanks to the work of a few dedicated modern scholars, including Arno Poebel, Thorkild Jacobson, and Samuel N. Kramer. Kramer, who died in 1990, became particularly known for his many excellent translations of Sumerian phrases and literature. According to a leading scholar who wrote his obituary:

In 1930, Dr. Kramer began the work that continued the rest of his life, excavating Sumerian tablets in Iraq and translating those, along with others from collections in Istanbul and at the University of Pennsylvania. . . .

Dr. Thorkild Jacobsen, [of] Harvard University, said Dr. Kramer was one of the rare scholars whose contribution to his field was "so basic that the field may be said to have been completely transformed, almost created, by him." . . .

In scholarly articles and some 30 books . . . , Dr. Kramer portrayed the Sumerians as people not very different from those in modern societies. They worked hard to earn a living, worried about their children, . . . and did not like to pay taxes. He discovered and enjoyed quoting one of their proverbs: "You can have a lord, you can have a king, but the man to fear is the tax collector."

John Noble Wilford, "Samuel Noah Kramer, 93, Dies; Was Leading Authority on Sumer," *New York Times*, November 27, 1990. http://query.nytimes.com/gst/fullpage.html?res=9C0CEFD71731F934A15752C1A966958260.

The Languages of Ancient Mesopotamia

Ubaidian	• One of the main ancient languages of the early Mesopotamian people
Sumerian	• Contains some words of Ubadian origin • Replaced older languages in the southern regions by the end of the fourth millennium B.C. • First language to achieve widespread use both verbally and in writing • Use as a spoken language declined by the early second millennium B.C.
Akkadian	• One of several Semitic languages originating from the western regions that ultimately replaced Sumerian • Became the chief language for business and correspondence by the mid-second millennium B.C. • Dialects that developed included Assyrian in the north and Babylonian in the South
Elamite and Hurrian	• Regional languages spoken in Mesopotamia in the third and second millennia B.C.
Amorite and Aramaic	• Other Semitic languages introduced to Mesopotamia in the third and second millennia B.C. • Aramaic eventually became the dominant language in the region as trade in the Near East continued to expand
Old Persian	• Entered the region with the conquests of Persian kings in the late 500s B.C.
Greek	• Used after Alexander the Great conquered the Persians in the late 300s B.C.
Arabic	• Semitic language that became dominant after the Islamic conquest in the seventh century A.D.

same importance as a unifying force that was later enjoyed in the same region by [another Semitic tongue,] Arabic, which displaced [Aramaic and other local languages] after the Islamic conquest in the seventh century A.D."[20]

In addition to Aramaic, two other languages later rose to prominence in ancient Mesopotamia (though neither proved as important as Aramaic or Arabic). One, Old Persian, circulated widely during the conquests of the first few Persian kings in the late 500s B.C. The other, Greek, came into use after Alexander the Great conquered the Persian Empire in the late 300s B.C.

Evolution of Cuneiform

The primary systems that developed to record these languages were of two basic types—complex, nonalphabetic ones and simpler, alphabetic ones. The main nonalphabetic system may have been partially based on a rudimentary mode of communication that came into use in the Near East as early as the eighth millennium B.C. It required small clay tokens similar to cylinder seals. Farmers and merchants may have pressed the tokens into wet clay, creating marks that stood for sheep, bushels of grain, and other commodities. Appropriately, eight "sheep marks" indicated eight sheep.

Sometime in the late 3000s B.C., the Sumerians introduced a more sophisticated form of writing, apparently first used in the city of Uruk. Modern scholars call it "cuneiform," after the Latin word *cuneus*, meaning wedge- or nail-shaped.

A tiny clay tablet contains information written in cuneiform on tracking inventory for a business.

This name comes from the fact that people who were trained to read and write pressed pointed sticks or other objects into moist clay tablets, producing little wedge-shaped marks. When the tablets dried and hardened, they became the world's first versions of books, account sheets, letters, historical records, religious literature, and so forth. There were between five hundred and six hundred separate cuneiform signs. These took a lot of time and effort to differentiate and memorize.

Another reason why cuneiform was hard to master was that it was considerably more complex than the older system of sheep marks and bushel marks. Early Sumerian cuneiform did use some picture signs. But it also employed homophony,

An early example of cuneiform on a tablet from around 2300 B.C. conveys a description of hitching donkeys to a plow through a combination of picture signs and sound signs.

in which some marks stood for sounds used in speech. To create a sentence, therefore, one had to combine picture signs and sound signs in complicated ways. Moreover, as time went on, the cuneiform signs, or script, became more abstract. For instance, the picture sign for a fish rotated 90 degrees so that it no longer looked anything like a fish, yet it still stood for a fish.

Despite its complexity, cuneiform was very useful, partly because it was easy to adapt to non-Sumerian tongues. "Cuneiform script could be employed to set down languages of any type," says Starr. "Both Semitic dialects [and] Indo-European tongues like Hittite and Old Persian were so written." But cuneiform's complexity did have the drawback of discouraging widespread literacy, as Starr explains:

> The number of individual signs was much larger than in an alphabetic form of writing [and] each of these [signs], though considerably simplified over the years, remained so complicated that only professional scribes [specially trained readers and writers] commonly wrote in the ancient Near East. Writing was an arcane [obscure and cryptic] mystery down to Greek times.[21]

In addition to Sumerian, Old Persian, and Hittite, other Near Eastern languages that utilized cuneiform scripts included Elamite, Hurrian, Babylonian, and Assyrian.

Deciphering Cuneiform

Although learning cuneiform was a difficult task for ancient Mesopotamian scribes, at least they had teachers (older scribes) to guide them. In contrast, early modern scholars who sought to decipher the ancient cuneiform scripts had no guides, either verbal or written. So their task was particularly difficult and tricky and required several years of joint effort.

That immense undertaking began in the A.D. 1760s and 1770s. Karsten Niebuhr, a Danish-born German surveyor and mathematician, took part in an expedition sponsored by the Danish king. The goal was to explore Mesopotamia and other parts of the Near East, which at the time Europeans saw as mysterious and exotic. Eventually, Niebuhr made it to the ancient Persian capital of Persepolis (in southern Iran). There, he found and examined ancient inscriptions written in three separate kinds of cuneiform script. Carefully, sign by sign, he copied the inscriptions into his notebooks, and in 1788 he published them.

One of scholars who read Niebuhr's manuscript was German philologist (language expert) Georg F. Grotefend. Fascinated, he tackled the job of deciphering the script having the fewest number of individual signs, and by 1802 he could read about a third of them. It was now clear that this cuneiform script represented Old Persian. Most of the rest of the signs in the Old Persian inscription were deciphered in the 1830s and 1840s by the brilliant British scholar, soldier, and diplomat Henry C. Rawlinson.

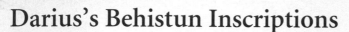

Darius's Behistun Inscriptions

In the inscriptions carved into the cliff face of the Behistun Rock, Persia's King Darius I bragged about the lands and peoples he had conquered. Part of his statement is translated here:

Kation Darius says: These are the countries which are subject to me. By the grace of [the Persian god] Ahura-mazda, they became subject to me; they brought tribute unto me. Whatsoever commands have been laid on them by me, by night or by day, have been performed by them.

King Darius says: Within these lands, whosoever was a friend, him have I surely protected. Whosoever was hostile, him have I utterly destroyed. By the grace of Ahura-mazda these lands have conformed to my decrees. As it was commanded unto them by me, so was it done. King Darius says: Ahura-mazda has granted unto me this empire. Ahura-mazda brought me help, until I gained this empire. By the grace of Ahura-mazda do I hold this empire.

Quoted in Livius, "The Behistun Inscription." www.livius.org/be-bm/behistun/behistun03.html.

Rawlinson next set his sights on decoding the other two scripts that Niebuhr had copied in Iran. In addition, another set of three distinct cuneiform inscriptions also came to Rawlinson's attention. These had been discovered on the Behistun Rock, the huge cliff on which the artisans of Persia's King Darius I had carved scenes of that monarch humiliating his enemies. Rawlinson journeyed to Behistun and immediately encountered a serious problem. Namely, the inscriptions lay some 328 feet (100m) up, in a place that was dangerous to reach even by the best rock climbers. Being young and athletic, however, he managed to get to the lower levels of inscriptions. "Later," as Kramer tells it,

he had himself suspended by a rope while he worked. He also used a ladder, balancing it on narrow ledges, while supporting himself perilously atop [the ladder] as he made copies of the symbols. The greatest difficulty came in recording [the topmost script because] it was so far out of reach on the vertical [cliff] face. . . . To get the work done, he finally hired a native Kurdish boy who inched his way across the smooth surface, somehow clinging to it with his fingers and toes, [and] while Rawlinson gave directions from below, the boy [recorded] the script.[22]

Having gained access to the three scripts, Rawlinson began examining them. He realized that one was written in the Old Persian form of cuneiform he was already familiar with. The second script, he surmised, must have been written in the tongue of ancient Babylon, because the same cuneiform signs it used had been discovered on the walls of that city. This turned out to be the Babylonian dialect of Akkadian. "Decipherment of the Old Persian version gave him the general sense and a number of proper names," Saggs explains.

Using this and new inscriptions [he] had taken major steps toward

British scholar Henry C. Rawlinson decoded the text found on the Behistun Rock and other examples of Old Persian, Akkadian, and Babylonian versions of cuneiform, allowing researchers to further piece together the details of ancient Mesopotamian languages and history.

the decipherment of Akkadian cuneiform by 1849. Other scholars were working on the script, and it quickly became possible to make out the sense of long texts and to begin to recover the details of the ancient history of the two main kingdoms in the area in the first and second millennia B.C., Babylonia and Assyria.[23]

Among the other scholars who had begun studying the scripts was Ireland's Edward Hincks. By 1851, he and Rawlinson had deciphered more than two hundred signs of the Babylonian script. Aided by German scholar Julius Oppert and British scholar William Talbot, Rawlinson and Hincks demonstrated that Assyrian was another dialect of

Akkadian. They also concluded that the third inscription found at Behistun was in Elamite, though they were unable to decipher it. That goal was achieved by other diligent scholars in the mid-twentieth century.

A New Window into History

The decipherment of the cuneiform scripts allowed modern scholars to read the contents of many thousands of surviving clay tablets produced by the Sumerians, Babylonians, Assyrians, Persians, and other ancient Mesopotamian peoples. Inscriptions in Sumerian cuneiform, which had long looked like chicken scratchings, now became readable. Among them were hymns to the gods, odes to rulers, school texts, and

Cuneiform Preserves Long-Dead Cultures

To date, more than half a million cuneiform tablets have been found in Mesopotamia and other parts of the Near East. The writings on these tablets have preserved revealing snapshots of various aspects of the ancient cultures of the region (including those of the Sumerians, Babylonians, Assyrians, and Persians). Large numbers of the tablets contain administrative and financial records, including inventories, bills, volumes of grain or other foodstuffs, and measures of

land parcels. These tell a great deal about economic practices, especially those of members of the upper classes, who owned the land and controlled commerce. Other cuneiform tablets preserve law codes and decrees issued by kings. And still others contain literature, including myths, hymns to the gods, tales of human heroes, odes commemorating the deeds of kings, lamentations for the fall of cities and rulers, wedding songs, and proverbs and wise sayings.

wise proverbs composed by Sumerian scribes more than four thousand years ago. As translated by Kramer, one of these proverbs reads: "If you take the field of an enemy, the enemy will come and take your field."[24]

In addition, the ability to read Akkadian cuneiform gave modern investigators a new window into the history of Babylonia and Assyria and the deeds of their rulers. The laws of one of those kings, Hammurabi of Babylon, could now be understood and translated into modern languages. In this way, for instance, it became clear what happened to someone who aided the escape of a slave in Hammurabi's kingdom: "If any one take a male or female slave of the court, or a male or female slave of a freed man, outside the city gates, he shall be put to death."[25]

The military exploits of the warlike Assyrian kings, also set down in Akkadian cuneiform, became readable as well. This permitted historians to piece together at least partial histories of the reigns of these monarchs. In a sense, their long-stilled voices could be heard again, as in the vivid boasts of King Shalmaneser I (reigned ca.1274–1245 B.C.) that he had defeated his Armenian and Hittite enemies:

I surrounded [them]. [They] cut off the passes and my water supply. Because of thirst and fatigue my army bravely advanced into the masses of their troops, and I fought a battle and accomplished

The ability to read the inscriptions on artifacts such as this stele containing King Hammurabi's law code greatly advanced researchers' knowledge of ancient Mesopotamian history.

their defeat. I killed countless numbers. . . . I cut down their hordes, [and] 14,400 of them I overthrew and took as living captives. Nine of [their] strongholds [and their] capital city I captured. . . . I slaughtered [them] like sheep.[26]

Even more personal and revealing were the contents of a series of letters written in cuneiform by various Mesopotamian and other Near Eastern kings in the late second millennium B.C. They are called the Amarna letters after the place in Egypt where they were discovered. In one of the more memorable ones, Burnaburiash, king of Babylonia, complains to Egypt's ruler that several Babylonian merchants had been robbed and killed in Palestine, which at the time was under Egyptian control:

To Akhenaten, King of Egypt, my brother. Thus speaks Burnaburiash King of Babylon, your brother. [Let me talk about] my merchants who traveled [in Palestine] for business. [Men working for a local ruler] beat my merchants and stole their money. [Palestine] is your country and its kings are your slaves. [I ask you to] bind them and return the money they robbed. And the men who murdered my slaves, kill them and avenge their blood. Because if you do not kill these men, they will again murder my caravans and even my ambassadors, and the ambassadors between us will cease.[27]

Easier Writing Systems

The second basic kind of writing system that came to be used in ancient Mesopotamia—the alphabetic variety—developed primarily because cuneiform was so complicated and hard to learn. Some people wanted to find an easier way to express themselves in writing. The most logical approach appeared to be an alphabet in which each sign stood for a specific sound made by people when they speak. Humans are able to produce relatively few separate and distinct sounds. Therefore, such a system will have considerably fewer sound signs, or what came to be called letters, than the combined picture signs and sound signs of cuneiform.

Two different scripts made up solely of such letters were introduced in the thirteenth century B.C. or not long afterward in Syria-Palestine. One, featuring about thirty or so letters, originated in the thriving port city of Ugarit. The other script, which had about twenty letters, was invented by the Phoenicians, a prosperous maritime people whose cities were situated farther down the Mediterranean coast from Ugarit. A few centuries later, the Greeks borrowed the Phoenician alphabet, which lacked vowel sounds. (Sometimes two or more Phoenician words had the same combination of consonants; the reader was expected to discern the word's meaning from the context of the sentence.) The Greeks added a few vowel sounds. The resulting alphabet became the basis for most later European versions, including those used today.

Meanwhile, the Aramaeans, who had originated in Syria's remote backcountry and migrated into Mesopotamia, began using an alphabetic script somewhat similar to the Phoenician version. With this script, the Aramaeans managed to write down their own Semitic tongue, Aramaic. Like the Greek version of the Phoenician script, the Aramaeans' alphabet featured vowels. Written Aramaic

A stone marker from the seventh to sixth centuries B.C. contains inscriptions in both Phoenician and Greek and shows an early example of alphabetic writing, in which signs (letters) stand for specific sounds.

was far simpler and easier to learn than any of the existing cuneiform scripts. Consequently, Aramaic became widely popular in the early first millennium B.C. and for a long time to come served as the lingua franca (universal tongue) of Mesopotamia and most of the rest of the Near East. According to Saggs:

> With Aramaeans present across the whole region from Syria to Babylonia, and some of them engaged in international trade, the Aramaic language was particularly appropriate for commercial documents and international correspondence. It had the additional advantage that the Aramaic writing system could be mastered in months, instead of the years needed for cuneiform. Even in some circles where cuneiform had always predominated, Aramaic writing was being used as a supplementary system soon after the middle of the eighth century B.C. . . . Thus, a cuneiform letter sent to [a] king [in] about 720 B.C. said it accompanied "a sealed Aramaic document," which must have been a full report to which the cuneiform letter served as an introduction.[28]

Thus, by the middle of the first millennium B.C., when the Assyrian Empire fell and the Persian Empire rose in its place, many different forms of writing had developed in Mesopotamia and neighboring regions. With these valuable tools, the peoples of these areas communicated among themselves. They also created snapshots of their cultures that would end up withstanding the ravages of time and becoming extremely valuable to modern observers.

Chapter Four

SCRIBES AND EDUCATION

It has been established that the first Mesopotamian writing systems, which remained in use for thousands of years, were very complex and difficult to master. One major result was that few people in the region were either literate or educated. For that reason, the writing process became largely the special privilege of an elite group of individuals—the scribes. They also mastered the use of a variety of different writing materials and tightly controlled the educational process. Out of a respect for tradition and a love of learning, the scribes of one generation proudly passed literacy and knowledge on to the next. It may be that few of them realized that at the same time they were making it possible for people born many thousands of years later to know who the ancient Mesopotamians were and what they did.

Jobs and Duties of Scribes

The Sumerians called a scribe a *dubsar*. Later, the Babylonians and Assyrians used the word *tupsharru* to denote such a person. Whatever people called them, scribes held important positions throughout the upper levels of Mesopotamian society. In palaces and government offices, for example, they kept records of supplies stored and used and wrote down diplomatic letters, decrees, and laws dictated to them by kings and other high officials.

Scribes who lived and worked on temple estates (the extensive lands and workshops owned and run by many temples) apparently performed even more wide-ranging duties. They copied traditional religious texts, acted as secretaries to the high priests, and kept records of the estates' workers and the commodities they produced. Also, Gwendolyn Leick

Scribes were charged with creating records for government, business, religious leaders, and private citizens. These four tablets, created by scribes in the mid-third millennium B.C., *contain contract language in the Akkadian form of cuneiform.*

points out, the traditional religious rituals that occurred in the temples "involved the recitation of [sacred] songs, hymns and incantations [magical words], and there was also a demand for specially commissioned literary works to commemorate the dedication of statues or the restoration of buildings by [kings]. All these services depended on a large number of literate [scribes]."[29]

Some evidence suggests that selected scribes might also have been assigned certain supervisory duties on such estates (perhaps because they were widely seen as respectable and responsible individuals). In a surviving exchange between a scribe and an estate superintendent, the scribe describes some of his own duties: "You have put me in charge over your house and never have I let you find me idling about. I held the [slaves] and the rest of [the workers in] your household to their tasks; [I] saw to it that they enjoyed their bread, clothing, [and] that they work properly. [I] made the men work [in the fields], a challenging task."[30]

Also, some scribes kept financial records for well-to-do private businesses. Their duties included keeping track of funds collected and spent; all supplies bought, used, and stored; and profits and losses. In addition, many scribes copied and added to existing scientific texts and lists. This made them ancient versions of modern mathematicians and astronomers (although at the time the sciences were not yet separate fields of endeavor or established professions). Finally, scribes were teachers who taught younger scribes and a few members of the upper classes how to read and write.

High Social Status

Thus, there were several different kinds of scribes in Mesopotamian society, with a wide range of duties. And the main attribute they had in common, and that set them apart from most other people, was that they were literate and educated. For that reason, one noted modern scholar, Yale University's Albrecht Goetze, suggested that the word *dubsar* did not denote any specific scribal profession. Rather it might have designated a general but special sort of social status or level of respectability. A modern equivalent, said Goetze, would be someone placing terms such as *Esquire* or *PhD* (doctor of philosophy) after his or her name to indicate a high level of education.

Whatever the word *scribe* denoted, there is no doubt that scribes enjoyed widespread respect and social status in Sumerian, Babylonian, Assyrian, and other societies. In fact, scribes were sometimes even politically influential.

After all, many of the close advisors to kings and generals were educated men who had attended scribal schools. Occasionally, in fact, a scribe actually rose to the position of royal monarch. Assyria's King Ashurbanipal (reigned ca. 668–627 B.C.), for example, originally trained as a scribe and actually copied some of the many literary texts in his vast palace library. One of his surviving inscriptions reads: "I studied the secret lore of the entire scribal craft. [I] have read intricate tablets inscribed with obscure Sumerian and Akkadian [texts, which are] difficult to unravel, and examined sealed, obscure, and confused inscriptions on stone from [the dim past]."[31]

The respectable social position of scribes is also evident from their background. Almost all scribal trainees were the sons of well-to-do or prominent members of the community. "Their fathers were governors," Nemet-Nejat writes, or "ambassadors, temple administrators, military officers, sea captains, important tax officials, priests, managers, accountants, foremen, and scribes, in other words, the wealthier citizens of the city."[32]

But though the majority of scribes were male, evidence shows that a few women either became scribes or received an education. The nunlike female devotees of the Mesopotamian sun god Shamash (or Utu), for instance, performed scribal duties in their own temples. Also, Enheduanna, daughter of the famous Akkadian king Sargon the Great, became highly literate and educated. After her father installed her as high priestess of the temple of the moon god (Nanna) at Ur, she wrote numerous poems and odes, some of which have survived.

Scribal Schools

Young people from prominent Mesopotamian families who aspired to become scribes attended special schools. The Sumerians called such a school an *edub-*

King Ashurbanipal, depicted directing his royal chariot in this limestone relief, was originally trained as a scribe. Because they were educated and literate, scribes in general enjoyed a high level of influence and esteem in ancient Mesopotamian society.

ba, meaning "tablet house," a reference to the clay tablets the students often wrote on. (The Akkadian word for a scribal school was *bit tuppi*). The first positively identified Mesopotamian schools were those established by the Sumerian king Shugli, who ruled Ur and its empire from around 2094 to 2047 B.C. However, some evidence shows that such schools existed in the region well before this time. For example, lists of vocabulary words clearly meant for students were discovered in the ruins of the Sumerian city of Uruk and dated to around 3000 B.C.

Some scribal schools may have existed in temples and palaces, although to date little evidence for them has been found. The vast majority of the remains of student tablets and other learning materials have been unearthed in rooms in large private houses. Such a school was excavated at Mari, long a prosperous city-state on the upper reaches of the Euphrates River. It had two rooms, one of which featured mud-brick benches. Experts estimate that two to four students sat at each bench. The walls are now mostly gone, but they once held shelves on which the students stacked their writing materials and daily exercises. An unusually large number of schools existed in private houses in Nippur, a southern Mesopotamian city renowned as a center of learning. Most of these houses had central courtyards, in which archaeologists have found benches for students and numerous tablets inscribed with writing exercises.

Such schools seem to have been open twenty-four days a month. On the other days, the students and teachers celebrated religious holidays or took what would now be called vacation time. The average school day lasted from early morning to sundown.

Respect and Strict Discipline

The headmaster and top-ranking scribe in an ancient Mesopotamian school was called the *ummia,* or "school father." He and the other teachers commanded great respect, both in school and in society, because they had attained a high level of learning. One surviving tablet contains a passage in which a student tells his teacher, "You have opened my eyes as though I were a puppy. You have formed humanity within me." A different section of the same text explains in more detail why the student felt he owed his teacher respect and loyalty:

The teacher assigned a task to me. It was a man's work. Like a springing reed, I leapt up and put myself to work. I did not depart from my teacher's instructions, and I did not start doing things on my own initiative. My mentor was delighted with my work on the assignment. He rejoiced that I was humble before him and he spoke in my favor. . . . He guided my hand on the clay and kept me on the right path. He made me eloquent with words and gave me advice. He focused my eyes on the rules which guide a man with a task. . . . He did not [show off]

An Argument Between Scribes

Students in ancient Mesopotamian scribal schools got into arguments and fights just as modern students do. Part of the proof for this is a surviving Sumerian text titled "School Rowdies." A trainee scribe named Enkimansi clashes with a classmate, Girnishag, over who is the better student.

Enkimansi: You dolt, numskull, school pest, you illiterate, you Sumerian ignoramus, your [writing] hand is terrible. It cannot even hold the [pen] properly. It is unfit for writing and cannot take dictation.

Girnishag: When you write a document it makes no sense. When you write a letter, it is illegible [unreadable]. . . . You are one of the most incompetent tablet writers. What are you fit for? Can anyone say? . . . Me, I was raised on Sumerian. I am the son of a scribe. But you are a bungler, a windbag.

Quoted in Samuel N. Kramer, *The Sumerians: Their History, Culture, and Character*. Chicago: University of Chicago Press, 1971, pp. 241–43.

his knowledge. His words were modest. If he had [bragged about] his knowledge, people would have frowned. . . . Once you have come into contact with such great brains, you will make your own words more worthy. . . . There, I have recited to you what my teacher revealed, and you . . . should pay attention. Taking it to heart will be to your benefit![33]

Although the *ummia* and other teachers were respected, they were also sometimes feared by their students. This was because these authority figures strictly enforced proper behavior and, when they deemed it necessary, employed corporal punishment (beatings). Evidence for this comes from a surviving text titled "Schooldays," written by a scribe circa 2000 B.C. Using memories of his own days as a student in an *edubba* as a model, he describes a boy going off to school carrying the lunch his mother had given him. Arriving late, which was frowned on, he stood before the headmaster "afraid and with pounding heart." The tardy student "made a respectful curtsy." But it was no use. The *ummia* beat him soundly with a stick, and more thrashings ensued as the day wore on: "My headmaster read my tablet and said: 'There is something missing,' [and then he] beat me. The fellow in charge of neatness said: 'You loitered in the street and did not straighten up your clothes,' [and he also] beat me. The fellow in charge of silence said: 'Why did you talk without permission?' [and he also] beat me."[34] The beatings continued in the days to come. Finally, the boy persuaded his father to invite the headmaster over for dinner, after which the beatings ceased.

Subjects Studied

In addition to running the school and enforcing discipline, the headmaster made sure the assistants, the scribal instructors, were doing their jobs. They specialized in assorted subject areas, much as modern high school and college teachers do. Thus, a scribe of counting taught the students arithmetic. And a scribe of Sumerian showed them how to read and write that language.

In fact, learning to write down languages must have occupied much of the

A clay tablet contains the schoolwork of a student studying to become a scribe in the early second millennium B.C.

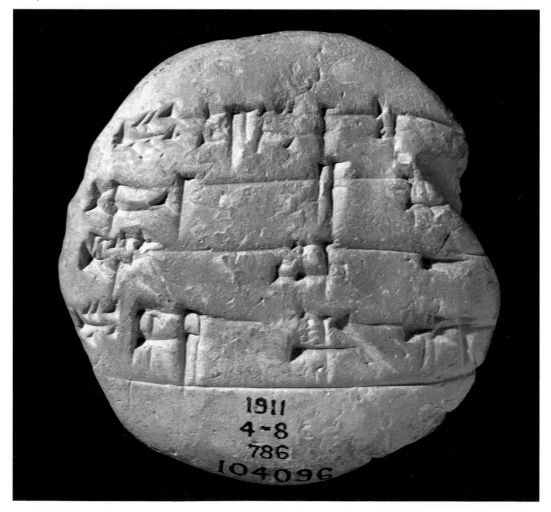

student scribes' time. For many centuries, writing Sumerian was an absolute must for scribes, so much so that any scribe who could not do so was subject to ridicule. "A scribe who does not know Sumerian, what kind of a scribe is he?" went one common proverb. Another asserted: "He is a deaf fool when it comes to the scribal art, a silent idiot when it comes to Sumerian."[35] Learning languages became even more complicated for young scribes when other languages besides Sumerian became widely used in Mesopotamia. Beginning in the late third millennium B.C., for example, the students had to learn both Sumerian and Akkadian. Later, some scribal schools required students to master Elamite, Persian, or other tongues as well and to translate one language into the others.

In addition to learning languages and arithmetic, trainee scribes became intimately familiar with existing literary works. These included, among others, Sumerian and other Mesopotamian epic poems, religious texts and hymns, decrees and historical records issued by kings, and traditional proverbs. The shorter works, along with hefty sections of the longer ones, were committed to memory. This is because the primary method of teaching was rote—constant repetition, both by writing and reciting the words, sentences, or paragraphs. The students copied and recopied these respected literary texts until they knew them by heart.

However, scribal teachers also created school texts of their own, which the student scribes copied and recopied to practice grammar and vocabulary. Some of these exercises have survived, including several that describe common activities and experiences within the schools—information that has aided modern scholars in reconstructing ancient Mesopotamian life. The following example summarizes a typical school day: "I recited my tablet, ate my food, prepared my new tablet, and wrote it out and completed it. . . . In the afternoon, my exercise tablets were brought to me. When school finished, I went home, went indoors, and found my father sitting there. I recited my tablet to him and he was highly pleased."[36]

Writing Materials

The writing tools and materials that student scribes used to do their exercises, and continued to use later when they became professionals, varied over time. One of the earliest, and for a long time the most common, writing surface was the clay tablet. A slab of moist clay was inexpensive and easy to write on. And when it dried and hardened, it lasted a long time. (It lasted even longer when it was baked in a fire or oven.)

Writing on such tablets became highly formalized over time, so that each tablet displayed certain standard features. In addition to the written message, list, or piece of literature, the scribe included a colophon—a mark that identified the tablet, him or her, or both. (Colophons were rare in early Mesopotamian writ-

Clay Tablets: Cheap and Durable

Which ancient Mesopotamian writing material was better? Experts say this question is hard to answer because each had its benefits. Certainly, as noted scholar A. Leo Oppenheim points out, clay tablets were the least expensive and most permanent:

Clay, which was used for the several cuneiform systems, happens to represent, especially when fired, the best—that is, the cheapest and most durable—writing material yet utilized by man, while papyrus, parchment, leather, wood, metal, and stone survive mainly by chance. Climatic conditions, the nature of the soil, and the ever-present human factor often wiped out such materials completely. Where the system of writing changed from one using clay to one for which more perishable materials were used, entire [historical] periods are blacked out for us. The disappearance of the last phases of Mesopotamian civilization is a good example of such a situation.

A. Leo Oppenheim, *Ancient Mesopotamia: Portrait of a Dead Civilization*. Chicago: University of Chicago Press, 1977, p. 229.

ings but appear frequently in later ones.) Often the colophon consisted of a catch-phrase, such as the work's first line. It was also common for scribes to write their names, creating a sort of signature. Many of these clay tablets were stored in archives, which have been found in the ruins of Mari, Nippur, Nineveh, and other ancient Mesopotamian cities. If someone wrote a personal letter on a tablet, he or she often put it in a dried clay container—the bulky equivalent of a modern envelope.

Scribes also learned to use wooden boards covered in wax, which, unlike hardened clay tablets, were reusable. The writer used a pointed wooden or metal tool to etch a message into the wax. He or she could later smooth out the wax or add fresh wax to erase the message and start over.

Of the many other writing materials that came into use in Mesopotamia, cylinder seals were also made of clay. Much larger were stelae, big slabs of stone or dried clay, on which rulers had scribes inscribe royal decrees or accounts of military conquests. For less formal messages and other writings, some people resorted to scribbling on ostraca, broken pieces of pottery, which were easy to come by and cheap. Other common writing surfaces included the faces of cliffs (like the Behistun Rock); the walls of palaces, temples, and other structures; and coffin lids.

An Egyptian text from approximately 500 to 300 B.C. is written on papyrus, a kind of paper made from a plant native to Egypt that was exported to and used in Mesopotamia. Because of their delicate composition and tendency to disintegrate with time, few papyrus-based texts from ancient times remain.

Although all of these writing materials and surfaces long remained in use across the Near East, another one eventually became more popular and widely used than most. It was papyrus, which became common in the first millennium B.C. Papyrus is a kind of paper made from a marsh plant native to Egypt. The Egyptians exported it to Mesopotamia and many other lands until the end of antiquity (ancient times). The first-century A.D. Roman scholar Pliny the Elder described the making of papyrus:

> Paper is manufactured from papyrus by splitting it [the plant's stem] with a needle into strips that are very thin but as long as possible. The quality of the papyrus is best at the center of the plant and decreases progressively toward the outsides. . . . All paper is "woven" on a board dampened with water from the Nile [to prevent the strips from drying out]; the muddy liquid acts as glue. First, an upright layer is smeared on the table—the whole length of the papyrus is used and both its ends are trimmed; then strips are laid across and complete a criss-cross pattern, which is then squeezed in presses. The sheets are dried in the sun and then joined together [by glue].[37]

The next step was to produce a papyrus roll. An artisan wound about twenty individual paper sheets around a wooden dowel, producing a roll 20 to 30 feet (6 to 9m) long. People wrote on the papyrus with a reed or bronze pen dipped in ink made from soot. Each papyrus roll, referred to in ancient times as a "book," contained about ten to twenty thousand words of text. The Assyrians, Aramaeans, Babylonians, Persians, Greeks, Romans, and several other peoples who inhabited or conquered Mesopotamia after around 1000 B.C. all used such rolls extensively. Unfortunately, because papyrus readily disintegrates over time, most of these writings have long since disappeared. So what little is known about ancient Mesopotamian scribes and the schools they attended comes from clay tablets and other older, more durable artifacts.

Chapter Five

EPIC POETRY

Ancient Mesopotamian civilization left behind a large, diverse, and rich assortment of literature, much of it of high quality. Examples of Sumerian writing from the late fourth millennium B.C.—in the form of cuneiform signs etched onto clay tablets—have survived; but these consist mostly of dry and repetitious administrative and financial records. The earliest surviving examples of actual literary works date from around 2400 B.C. And these are few in number. Most of the original versions of Sumerian literature have long since disappeared. The reason we know the stories told in some of these works is that the region's later peoples made copies, which fortunately have survived. As Nemet-Nejat tells it:

> The Babylonians and Assyrians imitated, revised, and translated Sumerian literature. [For that reason] Sumerian literature influenced Akkadian literature in style, viewpoint, and choice of subject. During the second half of the second millennium B.C., [Babylonian scribes] standardized many [earlier] literary works, [and] as texts were copied and recopied, the scribes sometimes edited the compositions by adding or deleting.[38]

Among the several literary genres that developed in early Mesopotamia, the longest, most detailed, and often most famous and beloved was epic poetry. The Sumerians produced numerous epic poems, which typically dealt with lofty themes. "The scale of an epic tapestry is broad," Bertman explains,

> for divine myth and heroic legend are the warp and woof [fabric] from which it is woven. Its themes

are the great deeds of human beings and the gods, and the intertwined existence of their worlds. Its length is often long, given the weight of its message, [including] the creation of the universe, the origins of heavenly beings and humanity, [and] the meaning and purpose of life.[39]

These epic tales are more than just well-written, entertaining examples of early literature. They also reveal a great deal about how the early peoples of Mesopotamia viewed themselves and their relationship with the gods and nature. In addition, they have a special appeal to Western observers today. This is because a number of characters, events, and themes of these works were later absorbed by the Hebrews, Greeks, and other ancient peoples whose cultures profoundly shaped Western civilization. A good example is the universal flood story that appears in more than one Sumerian epic. A later version of it was incorporated into the Hebrew scriptures, which became the Old Testament.

Origins of Gilgamesh's Story

The most important and famous of these epics was the story of the Sumerian hero Gilgamesh and his search for the secret of immortality. Babylonian scribes made copies of the original in around 2000 B.C. That original, like

A Fortunate Literary Discovery

Although the first English translation of the Epic of Gilgamesh *was accomplished in 1872 by English scholar George Smith, roughly fifteen of the poem's thirty-five hundred lines were still missing. Not long afterward, Smith led an expedition to Iraq to locate the lost lines. And in an extraordinary stroke of good fortune, he found them after digging for only a few weeks. Smith later recalled:*

I sat down to examine the store of fragments of cuneiform inscriptions from the day's digging, taking out and brushing off the earth from the fragments to read their contents. On cleaning one of them I found to my surprise . . . that it contained the greater portion of seventeen lines of inscription belonging to the first column of the [Babylonian] account of the Deluge [great flood], and fitting into the only place where there was a serious blank in the story. When I had first published the account of this tablet I had conjectured that there were about fifteen lines wanting [lacking] in this part of the story, and now with this portion I was enabled to make it nearly complete.

Quoted in C.W. Ceram, ed., *Hands on the Past: Pioneer Archaeologists Tell Their Own Story.* New York: Knopf, 1966, p. 250.

other written versions of epic poetry, was almost certainly based on an oral tradition that stretched back in time, perhaps even to the era before the Sumerians invented writing. Therefore, Nemet-Nejat says, "It is possible that generations of storytellers and scribes were involved in creating the final product."[40]

Part of the evidence that different storytellers helped shape different parts of Gilgamesh's story is that it was originally not a single tale. Several distinct minor Sumerian epics about Gilgamesh and his exploits existed in the third millennium B.C. Among them were *Gilgamesh and the Bull of Heaven; Gilgamesh, Enkidu, and the Netherworld; Gilgamesh and the Land of the Living;* and *The Death of Gilgamesh.* These small-scale works were later combined into one larger-scale epic poem. It had about three thousand lines, which were divided into twelve sections, each section carved on a separate cuneiform tablet. Roughly 80 percent of the text of this longer version was discovered in the ruins of King Ashurbanipal's library at Nineveh. It has become the standard version used in modern translations.

The main character of the epic may well have been a real Sumerian ruler. Surviving cuneiform lists of early Sumerian kings do mention a ruler named Gilgamesh who lorded over the city of Uruk circa 2700 B.C. Nothing of a historical nature is known about his reign. But his deeds were apparently memorable enough to inspire later generations of Mesopotamians to write minor epics about him.

A relief depicts the epic hero Gilgamesh, a character who may be based upon a real Sumerian king of the same name who ruled the city of Uruk around 2700 B.C.

Slaying the Giant

In Gilgamesh's story, he and his friend Enkidu battle the giant of the Cedar Mountain. Aiding the heroes, the god Shamash sends a powerful wind, which blows down many trees. The Babylonian version gives this description of the scene:

Hawawa fell to his knees [and] cried out: "I, Hawawa, [will become] your servant. I will cut down the trees for you. Shamash has blown me down. . . . Gilgamesh you are king of Uruk. I, Hawawa can guard the wood for Uruk's gates." Enkidu with a mighty roar did say: "The demon lies. He must be killed.". . . Gilgamesh did take heart from Enkidu's words [and] with his sword did slice into Hawawa's neck from the right [and] Enkidu . . . with his ax did chop into Hawawa's neck from the left. And Hawawa's tongue . . . spoke never more.

Quoted in MythHome, "The Tablets Telling the Epic of Gilgamesh, Tablet 5, Hawawa Defeated." www.mythome. org/gilgamesh5.html.

Whether or not Gilgamesh was a real person, his classic story examines several basic truths about humanity and its place in nature. Gilgamesh and his colorful companion, Enkidu, who are heroes of epic proportions, symbolize humanity as a whole as they search for these truths. As in Greek tragedy (which developed in Athens in the fifth century B.C.), the heroes come to question the meaning and value of human existence. And in search of answers, they turn to the gods or to wise old sages. One of these sages, Utnapishtim (or Atrahasis), is the Mesopotamian version of the biblical Noah, who supposedly saved humanity by building a huge ark. (In a story-within-the-story, Utnapishtim tells the tale of the great flood to Gilgamesh.)

Gilgamesh and the Wild Man

A brief summary of the plot of Gilgamesh's epic shows the skilled way in which the early Sumerian storytellers wove a complex narrative with universal themes and appeal. As the story begins, Gilgamesh is a formidable and fearless soldier and king. Yet he is also a conceited individual who cares little for other people's feelings, so in time the people of Uruk become fed up with him. The city's elders ask for help from the widely respected mother goddess, Aruru, who is Uruk's patron deity. She agrees to help.

Aruru's remedy is to create a rival for Gilgamesh, someone who is his equal in strength and fighting ability and who might teach him a lesson in humility. She goes to the riverbank and finds some moist clay. With this, she constructs a primitive man, named Enkidu, whose body is covered in hair. Enkidu begins wandering around the fields near the city and mingling with the cattle and other beasts.

It is not long before Gilgamesh hears about the wild man. The king orders someone to bring Enkidu to the royal palace in Uruk. As the months go by, servants cut the strange guest's hair, dress him in elegant clothes, and teach him table manners.

Gilgamesh's plan to civilize the wild man succeeds. But the king gets more than he bargained for. Because Aruru instilled in Enkidu a powerful sense of right and wrong and of justice, Enkidu becomes more civilized than Gilgamesh. This becomes evident one night as the king and Enkidu are strolling through the city. Gilgamesh is about to enter a house without being invited when Enkidu suddenly stands in his way, thereby provoking a knock-down, drag-out brawl. Here is the way it is described in the Babylonian version of the story:

Enkidu, [the] wild man, stood ready to meet and stop the king. Gilgamesh came [at him] like a wild ox [and] a struggle did begin. Each body on the other did meet with . . . heavy blows. Stray swings [of their fists] did the door break, did the door jamb break, and the walls did crack. On to the streets did the pair wrestle, wild heart to wild heart. Doors fell, corners [of walls] were

Cylindrical seals depict the exploits of Gilgamesh and Enkidu, his rival-turned-friend, after their epic clash.

In one part of the Gilgamesh epic, the sun god, Shamash, wants Gilgamesh and Enkidu to perform a heroic deed. This terracotta tablet depicts Gilgamesh and Enkidu killing Hawawa the giant, who has been terrorizing the Cedar Mountain.

broken off, stalls knocked down, and still on they fought. They fought to the city gates, which trembled with their blows.[41]

The battle ends in a draw. Gilgamesh is so astonished at encountering someone as strong and daring as he is that the two became close friends. Moreover, Enkidu sets a moral example for the king. Gilgamesh abandons his old, disreputable ways and becomes a just, caring ruler who is greatly admired by his subjects.

The gods, who have been watching the events in Uruk, are also pleased. One of their number, Shamash, the sun god, suggests that Gilgamesh and Enkidu perform a heroic deed, namely kill an evil giant. The monster, named Hawawa, has been terrorizing the land of the Cedar Mountain, situated west of the Mesopotamian plains. The two heroes journey to the Cedar Mountain and manage to slay Hawawa.

Gilgamesh and Enkidu are less fortunate in their dealings with another deity, however. Ishtar, goddess of love, tries to take Gilgamesh as a lover. But he refuses, and she retaliates by sending a giant bull to destroy Uruk. The heroes kill the bull, after which Ishtar inflicts a curse on Enkidu that causes him to become sick and die.

Searching for Immortality

Gilgamesh is overcome with grief over the death of his friend. At the same time, he expresses his puzzlement about and distress over the utter finality of death. This moment of human weakness is captured in a beautiful passage in the epic's eighth tablet: "Enkidu you are asleep. What has made you sleep? Great evil has taken Enkidu, my friend. Enkidu your flesh is rotting. Why is that? . . . Enkidu your eyes no longer move. Why is that? . . . Enkidu I cannot feel the beat of your heart. Why is that? Great evil has taken Enkidu my friend."[42]

While mourning Enkidu, Gilgamesh goes out into the desert and ponders the meaning and inevitability of death. For the first time in his life, he comes to grips with the realization that all living things, including himself, must someday pass away. And he begins to wonder if perhaps there might be some way to avoid this seemingly terrible fate. Then he is suddenly overcome by a flash of inspiration. In hopes of saving humanity from the curse of death, he must find the secret of eternal life.

At that moment, Gilgamesh remembers an old story about how the gods had bestowed immortality on a former Sumerian king, Utnapishtim, also known as Atrahasis, the "wise one." This old sage now lived far to the west on an island in the "Great Sea" (today called the Mediterranean). "I will seek out Utnapishtim to tell me how to avoid my death,"[43] Gilgamesh declares.

The determined young king wastes no time in embarking on a long and arduous trek to the sea. Along the way, he finds his way blocked by an army of hideous scorpion-men, who at first refuse to let him go any further. Using his wits, Gilgamesh explains the nature of his mission. If he is successful in finding the secret of immortality, he says, that knowledge will benefit the scorpion-men as much as it will humans. Hearing this, the creatures allow him to continue on his fateful journey.

Eventually, Gilgamesh reaches the sea, obtains a boat, and sails to the fabled island home of Utnapishtim. To the younger man's surprise, the older man knows full well who he is and why he has come. Utnapishtim proceeds to tell the tale of how he acquired the gift of eternal life. Long ago, the gods sent a giant flood to destroy the human race, and one of the deities warned Utnapishtim in advance and instructed him to build a big boat. The man brought his family aboard that vessel, along with representatives of all the living things in his world. Soon afterward, torrents of rain fell for six days and seven nights, causing an enormous flood that drowned all the people and animals that were not in the boat. After the catastrophe, one of the gods rewarded Utnapishtim for saving a vestige of humanity. That gift was immortality, which allowed him to survive for many centuries.

Having heard this incredible tale from the lips of the old sage, Gilgamesh demands to know the secret of eternal life. Utnapishtim tells him that it consists of a special flower one must eat to acquire immortality. That flower grows at the bottom of the sea, the old man warns, where no human can reach it.

But because Gilgamesh possesses strength and bravery beyond that of ordinary people, he is able to retrieve the miraculous flower. Determined to bring it to his people back in Uruk, he sets out for home. But when he is only a few miles from the city, he makes the mistake of putting the flower down for a

A series of tablets containing the story of Gilgamesh was discovered in the ruins at Nineveh. This piece is known as the Flood Tablet, depicting the hero's meeting with Utnapishtim as part of his quest for immortality.

moment, and a snake steals it. Gilgamesh has failed in his quest. But he has learned a valuable lesson that he can and must pass on to future generations. Only the gods are immortal, while people, no matter how strong, courageous, or good, must face death in the end.

The Creation Story

Another epic poem highly revered by the Sumerians, Babylonians, and several other ancient Mesopotamian peoples was the *Epic of Creation*. The Babylonians called it the *Enuma Elish*, based on its opening words, which translate into English as "when on high" (or "when in heaven"). Special performers recited the work aloud in public each year during Babylonia's New Year's festival. Earlier Sumerian versions of the story featured some key Sumerian gods, including An, Enlil, and Nammu. The Babylonian version featured the Babylonian equivalents of these deities—in particular, Marduk, supreme leader of Babylonia's pantheon (group of gods).

That Babylonian edition of the tale dates from the twelfth century B.C. and consists of about a thousand lines on seven cuneiform tablets. Like the Babylonian version of Gilgamesh's story, it was discovered in Ashurbanipal's library at Nineveh. The noted scholar George Smith published the first translation of the *Epic of Creation* in 1876.

Nearly everyone who read the translation immediately pointed out what they saw as eerie similarities between sections of the epic and the creation story that appears in the Old Testament's book of Genesis. Indeed, both stories deal with a divine being shaping the first humans in his own image. One important difference is that the sole god of Genesis fashions people on his own, for his own reasons; whereas in the Babylonian work the creation of humanity is one of several outcomes of a struggle among multiple gods.

As the *Epic of Creation* opens, Apsu, god of underground waters, and Tiamat, goddess of salt water, mate and give rise to several deities, who in turn produce still more gods. Eventually, there are so many heavenly beings that Apsu becomes annoyed by the incessant noise they make. He is tempted to kill most of them. However, Ea, the god of freshwater and wisdom, intervenes and overthrows Apsu. Soon afterward, Ea has a son, Marduk.

In time, Tiamat decides to punish Ea for deposing her mate, Apsu, and to that end she organizes an army of repulsive monsters. Their leader is Kingu. He controls the Tablet of Destinies, which lists the ultimate fates of all living things. Seeing the approach of this army, Ea enlists the aid of his son, Marduk, who has by this time become a mighty warrior. After Ea grants him the title "King of the Universe," Marduk puts on his armor and faces down the attacking monsters, who are so afraid of him that they run for their lives. Marduk then meets Tiamat in single combat and slays her. He also seizes the Tablet of Destinies from Kingu.

The victorious Marduk now engages in a series of impressive acts of creation. Cutting Tiamat's lifeless body in half, he uses part of it to make the sky. Marduk also creates the stars and the earth and announces that he will build a lovely temple there and call it Babylon. Hearing this, the other gods ask him: "Over all that your hands have created, who will have your authority? Over the ground which your hands have created, who will have your power?" This inspires Marduk to fashion a race of humans to inhabit the earth. "I will take blood and fashion bone," he says. "I will establish a savage, 'man' shall be his name. . . . He shall be charged with the service of the gods, that they might be at ease!"[44]

Other Important Epics

In addition to the epics about Gilgamesh's and Marduk's adventures, the ancient Mesopotamians composed other long works dealing with gods and human heroes. Most of these continued to show a mythical framework. The plots involved gods opposing and fighting other gods or people interacting with these deities and/or battling giants and other fanciful monsters.

Not until the late second millennium B.C. did Mesopotamian poets begin to write epics based firmly on historical characters and true events. Most of these came from Assyria and dealt with the conquests and other activities of powerful kings. The only epic of this type of which significant fragments have

This tablet is from a series containing the Epic of Creation *poem, from the ruins at Nineveh. Scholars have noted the similarities between this tale and the creation story of the book of Genesis from the Old Testament.*

survived is the *Tukulti-Ninurta Epic*. It celebrated the victory of King Tukulti-Ninurta I (reigned ca. 1244–1208 B.C.) over his Babylonian enemies.

It is important to note that neither the poet nor the king (acting within the story) neglects the gods. The epic ends with Tukulti-Ninurta staging a public display of faithfulness and giving a load of treasure (stolen from the Babylonians) to the temples of Assyria's gods. Indeed, it was simply unthinkable to suggest that

King Tukulti-Ninurta I, whose victory over his Babylonian rivals is captured in an ancient epic poem, is depicted making an offering to the gods in a relief from the Ishtar Temple in Ashur, dated 1220 B.C.

Trapped in the Underworld

Of the ancient Mesopotamian epics dealing with divine relationships, one of the most famous is *The Descent of Inanna*. It describes the goddess Inanna's adventures in the Underworld. The love goddess decides to visit her sister, Ereshkigal, queen of the Underworld, and Ereshkigal pretends to welcome Inanna. But because Ereshkigal is secretly jealous of her sister, she suddenly turns on and murders her. Fortunately for Inanna, some other gods intervene and manage to bring her back to life. However, a group of divine judges informs her that she is doomed to remain in the Underworld for eternity unless she can find a substitute who will take her place. Inanna eventually makes a deal with her lover, Dumuzi. Thereafter, he spends half of each year in the dark depths and she lives there during the other half. Most scholars believe that this epic inspired the later Greek myth of the goddess Persephone, who had to spend half of each year in the Underworld. Both tales demonstrate a powerful universal truth that many ancient peoples came to accept—namely, even the gods must follow certain rules governing life, death, and fate.

any person, even a king, could succeed in life without divine support. "Since the dawn of Mesopotamian history," scholar Enrico Ascalone points out, "the chief of the community established the rightfulness of his position through [his] belief that he had been chosen by the gods to watch over earthly life."[45] For that reason, the gods are ever-present authority figures in all ancient Mesopotamian epics.

Chapter Six

Sacred and Secular Literature

Although the Sumerians and other ancient Mesopotamian peoples are renowned for their epic poems, they produced many other literary works covering a wide range of subjects and styles. For the sake of convenience, these can be divided into two broad categories. The first is sacred literature, consisting of hymns, prayers, and letters written to various gods. The other category is secular, or nonreligious, literature. Major genres include laments (sad comments or songs), proverbs and other wise sayings, love poems, royal inscriptions, personal letters, medical and astrological texts, educational texts, and historical accounts.

Single examples of literary works in these genres have been found in the ruins of houses, palaces, temples, and other ancient buildings. However, most surviving examples come from archives, sometimes referred to as libraries. (The term *library* can be misleading because the peoples of ancient Mesopotamia did not have libraries in the modern sense, that is, public places that lent books to people.) Nemet-Nejat describes these ancient archives or libraries as "all records amassed at the time a particular task was carried out by an institution or person." Many personal libraries were accumulated by scribes who worked in schools, temples, or palaces, she explains.

Scholars often kept their private archives (for example, legal and administrative records) and professional libraries (such as school, literary, and scientific texts) together, as did the scribe at Ur who ran a school from his home in "Quiet Street no. 7." The majority of [surviving] information [and literature] from all periods comes from economic, administrative, and literary texts from temple and palace archives. These large institutions often had separate rooms for filing and storing records.[46]

One such large archive was discovered at Mari. It held thousands of texts, among them numerous letters written to and from Mari's rulers in the nineteenth century B.C. But the biggest ancient Mesopotamian library found so far is the one maintained by King Ashurbanipal at Nineveh. Unearthed in A.D. 1849 by British diplomat and archaeologist Austen Henry Layard, it originally contained more than twenty thousand tablets. Of these, more than five thousand have been translated.

Sacred Hymns and Prayers

Among the most abundant documents discovered in ancient archives and other places across Mesopotamia are sacred texts, especially hymns and prayers. A majority of the hymns were likely written by literate priests to be used in worship, initially by the priests themselves and eventually by ordinary citizens. "Once transcribed," Bertman points out, "the words of praise could then be copied and recited by others. Such songs of praise may have been accompanied by instrumental music."[47]

These hymns of praise to the gods are valuable to modern scholars because they both describe the deities, including their attributes and powers, and show the levels

Hymn to Inanna

Enheduanna, who served as high priestess of the moon god at Ur sometime shortly after 2300 B.C., is credited with composing a number of surviving hymnlike poems. This is an excerpt from one titled Inninsagurra, *or "Stout-Hearted Lady," dedicated to Inanna, goddess of love and passion:*

The Mistress, the stout-hearted, impetuous Lady, proudest among the Anunna-gods, surpassing in all lands [and] exalted among the "Great Princes," the queen performing great deeds. . . . she rivals the great [chief god] An, she is the august leader among the great gods, she makes their verdict final. . . .

. . . She holds a halter in her hand. . . . Her radiance covers the great mountain, silences the road. The gods of the land are panic-stricken by her heavy roar.

. . . To interchange the brute and strong and the weak and powerless is yours, Inanna. . . . To give the crown, the chair and the scepter of kingship is yours, Inanna.

Quoted in Other Women's Voices Before 1700 B.C., "Enheduanna." http://home.infionline.net/~ddisse/enheduan.html#anchor33888.

Among the hymns and prayers of ancient Mesopotamia that have been discovered are those involving the love goddess Inanna, depicted here in a relief.

of reverence and respect worshippers had for them. A good example is the following hymn to Enlil, whom the Sumerians and Babylonians saw as the divine ruler of the earth and bestower of kingship on humans. (The Babylonians called him Ellil.) It dates from the mid- to late third millennium B.C.

> Enlil! His authority is far-reaching, his word is sublime and holy.
>
> His decisions are unalterable, he decides fates forever! His eyes scrutinize [examine] the entire world! When the honorable Enlil sits down in majesty on his sacred and sublime throne . . . the other gods prostrate [lie flat on their faces] before him and obey his orders without protest! He

is the great and powerful ruler who dominates Heaven and Earth, who knows all and understands all![48]

Other Mesopotamian hymns and prayers resemble love songs. In part, this may be because people recited them in ceremonies in which kings married (ritually rather than literally) the love goddess Inanna. A number of modern scholars have suggested that these works inspired the Hebrew psalms in the Old Testament. For instance, a hymn of Shu-sin (reigned ca. 2037–2027 B.C.), one of the kings of the Ur III dynasty, reads in part:

> Bridegroom, let me caress you, my precious caress is sweeter than honey. In the bed-chamber, honey-filled, let

Hymn to a "Magnificent Lady"

The following excerpt is part of a Sumerian hymn to Inanna, goddess of love and passion:

The great-hearted mistress, the impetuous lady, proud among the gods and pre-eminent in all lands . . . the magnificent lady who gathers up the divine powers of heaven and earth and rivals great An, is mightiest among the great gods—she makes their verdicts final. . . . Her great awesomeness covers the great mountain and levels the roads.

At her loud cries, the gods of the Land become scared. . . . Wherever she [goes], cities become ruin mounds and haunted places, and shrines become waste land.

Quoted in Electronic Text Corpus of Sumerian Literature, "A Hymn to Inanna." http://etcsl.orinst.ox.ac.uk/cgi-bin/etcsl.cgi?text=t.4.07.3&charenc=j#.

me enjoy your goodly beauty. Lion, let me caress you. . . . Your spirit, I know here to cheer your spirit. Bridegroom, sleep in our house until dawn. Your heart, I know where to gladden your heart. Lion, sleep in our house until dawn.[49]

Proverbs and Fables

Almost as prevalent as hymns in ancient Mesopotamian literature and society were proverbs—short, wise sayings that people handed down from one generation to the next. At first, this transmission was strictly oral. But sometime in the second millennium B.C., scribes started keeping written collections of proverbs. Several of these collections have survived. One reason for the enduring popularity of proverbs was that the pace of change was extremely slow in Mesopotamian society. So people in each generation believed that the wisdom accumulated by their ancestors was still valuable and could be applied to their own situation.

In fact, this variety of so-called wisdom literature consistently captured basic truths of the human condition. For that reason, many ancient Mesopotamian proverbs have universal appeal to nearly all times and places, including Western society today. Take, for example, the proverb that stated: "The poor men are the silent men in Sumer."[50] It made the point that poor people typically had no political voice and were often taken for granted and ignored by members of the upper classes. That situation still prevails in most human societies.

Other parts of ancient Mesopotamian wisdom include: "If you take the field of an enemy, the enemy will come and take your field"; "Conceiving is nice, but pregnancy is irksome"; "For a man's pleasure there is marriage, while on thinking it over, there is divorce";[51] "One cannot drag out the weak [and] one cannot hold back the strong"; and "He who insults is insulted, [while] he who sneers is sneered at."[52]

Another popular kind of wisdom literature in ancient Mesopotamia consisted of brief, humorous tales, or fables. Each satirized, or poked fun at, a common social situation, especially one involving some sort of inequity or injustice. In one widely repeated example, a simple, uneducated gardener proves that he has more common sense than a highly educated doctor. A large number of these fables involve talking animals that behave like people; they closely resemble and likely influenced the famous fables attributed to the Greek writer Aesop. The following example—a conversation between an elephant and a bird—makes the point that size and strength are not always superior qualities: "The elephant [said]: 'There is nothing like me among all the creatures. . . . The one that can defecate [poop] like me has yet to be created!' The [bird] answered him: 'But I, in my own small way, can defecate just as much as you.'"[53]

Expressions of Grief or Sadness

In contrast to the mostly lighthearted tone of the proverbs and fables, another ancient Mesopotamian literary genre—the lament—was serious, somber, and usually sad. Laments (or lamentations) were poems that commemorated the death of a person, often a king, or the fall of a city or nation. Many laments were either addressed to a god or asked the gods for forgiveness or mercy.

Because surviving laments typically describe how a person died or a city fell, they frequently have a certain amount of historical value. This is certainly the case with one of the earliest and most famous ancient Mesopotamian laments, the *Lamentation over the Destruction of Ur*. Dating from shortly after 2000 B.C., it was composed to mark the fall of the Sumerian empire now called the Third Dynasty of Ur, or Ur III. One section graphically captures the gruesome aftermath of war: "The roads were piled with dead. In the wide streets, where feasting crowds once gathered, jumbled they lay. In all the streets and roadways bodies lay. In open fields that used to fill with dancers, the people lay in heaps. The country's blood now filled its holes, like metal in a mold. Bodies dissolved like butter left in the sun."[54]

The Sumerian and other Mesopotamian laments strongly inspired the ones in the Bible's book of Lamentations. Written shortly after the capture of the Hebrew city of Jerusalem by the Babylonians, one passage reads: "The Lord [has] delivered into the hands of the enemy the walls of [Jerusalem's] palaces. . . . Cry aloud to the Lord! O daughter of Zion [Israel]! Let tears stream down like a torrent day and night! Give yourself no rest, your eyes no respite!"[55]

A tablet contains the text of the Lamentation over the Destruction of Ur, *a somber retelling of the Sumerian empire's demise dating from around 2000 B.C.*

Letters to Kings, Gods, and Parents

Among the more numerous examples of written literature in ancient Mesopotamia were letters, either carved onto clay tablets or written on animal hide, papyrus, or some other more perishable material. Whatever they were written on, these letters followed a standard, accepted form, as letters do today. Most modern letters start with a salutation such as "Dear X" or "Dear Mr. X." In contrast, a typical Mesopotamian salutation was "X says the following: Tell Y that . . .", or words to that effect. After the salutation, the letter writer said that he or she hoped the recipient was in good health, and then went on to the body of the letter.

The style and tone of such a letter often depended on the social status of the letter writer and recipient. If the letter writer was a member of a lower social class than the recipient, the writer took a submissive tone and used phrases such as "I grovel at your feet." If the two people were social equals, the letter writer addressed the recipient as "brother." And if the writer had a higher social status than the recipient, the letter's tone might be very direct, firm, or even harsh.

Among the many surviving ancient Mesopotamian and Near Eastern letters, a large number consist of exchanges among kings and other rulers. A particularly large and rich collection of such royal correspondence was discovered in Mari's archive. It includes personal letters written by the early Assyrian king Shamshi-Adad (reigned ca. 1813–1781 B.C.) to his sons (and their answers to him). Numerous other Assyrian royal letters were found in the ruins of Ashurbanipal's library at Nineveh.

It was also customary for the ancient Sumerians, Babylonians, Assyrians, and their Near Eastern neighbors to write letters to the gods. Some of these documents were dictated by kings and read aloud to their assembled subjects by scribes or heralds. The king usually expressed his thanks to a god for granting divine help (such as ending a drought) or asked for guidance during a crisis. Ordinary people also had scribes write letters to various gods in hope that the deities would heal them or their relatives or friends. In the following example, a Sumerian woman addresses the goddess Nintinuga (or Gula), who oversaw medicine and healing:

> Say to Nintinuga, the physician of the Land . . . the merciful and compassionate one who listens to prayers. You are the caretaker of the living and the dead; you are the great healer of all the crippled ones. This is what Inanaka, [your] maidservant, says: I have fallen ill for a second time. . . . I have no one who would take care of me [and] I am distressed. If it pleases my lady . . . may the [illness-causing] demon which is in my body leave my body. [If you heal me] I will then be[come] the courtyard sweeper of your temple and will serve you.[56]

Family members also exchanged letters, in which they discussed personal

Good Advice for Farmers

Among the various kinds of wisdom literature popular in ancient Mesopotamia were short works giving advice on how best to perform certain common tasks. This example deals with proper farming tools and techniques.

Your implements should be ready. The parts of your yoke should be assembled. Your new whip should hang from a nail—the bindings of the handle of your old whip should be repaired by artisans.

The adze [ax], drill and saw, your tools, and your strength, should be in good order. Let braided thongs, straps, leather wrappings, and whips be attached securely. Let your sowing basket be checked, and its sides made strong. What you need for the field should be at hand. Inspect your work carefully.

Quoted in Electronic Text Corpus of Sumerian Literature, "The Farmer's Instructions." http://etcsl.orinst.ox.ac.uk/cgi-bin/etcsl.cgi?text=t.5.6.3&charenc=j#.

needs and concerns. The following example was written by a Babylonian student named Iddin-Sin to his mother in the eighteenth century B.C.

Tell the Lady Zinu: Iddin-Sin sends the following message:

May the gods [keep] you forever in good health for my sake.

From year to year, the clothes of the young gentlemen here become better, but you let my clothes get worse from year to year. Indeed, you persisted in making my clothes poorer and more scanty. . . . [My classmate] the son of Adad-iddinam . . . has two new sets of clothes, while you fuss even about a single set of clothes for me. In spite of the fact that you [gave birth to] me and his mother only adopted him, his mother loves him, while you, you do not love me![57]

Historical Accounts

The art of systematic, detailed historical writing started in the fifth century B.C. in Greece, well after most of the major Mesopotamian civilizations had already come and gone. However, the ancient Mesopotamians did produce various writings that can be loosely viewed as historical accounts. The earliest of these were lists of kings and their reigns compiled by Sumerian scribes. The Babylonians and several other later Near Eastern peoples also kept king lists of their own royal dynasties. These lists

A tablet contains a chronological list of kings at the city of Larsa from 2025–1763 B.C., one of various ancient Mesopotamian writings that provide general accounts of history.

are neither complete nor accurate. The Sumerian king lists, for example, claim that certain rulers had reigns lasting tens of thousands of years.

Fortunately for modern historians, the reigns of the last few Assyrian and Babylonian kings can be dated with a fair amount of accuracy. In large degree this is thanks to the survival of two collections of historical documents—the *Babylonian Chronicles* and the records of the Assyrian kings. The *Babylonian Chron-*

icles date from the period beginning in the eighth century B.C. and ending in the second century B.C. They describe various military, political, and social events that occurred during that era. Though they are far from complete and unbiased, scholars find them very valuable when combined with other sources, such as the Assyrian royal records and some books of the Bible. The later and most detailed *Babylonian Chronicles* include the *Fall of Nineveh Chronicle*, the *Artaxerxes III Chronicle*, and the *Alexander the Great Chronicle*. This excerpt from the *Fall of Nineveh Chronicle* describes incidents in 612–611 B.C., when the Babylonians and Medes were attacking Assyria:

The king of [Babylonia] mustered his army and marched to Assyria. The king of the Medes [Cyaxares] marched towards the king of [Babylonia] and they met one another. . . . The king of [Babylonia] and his army crossed the Tigris; Cyaxares had to cross the Radanu [River], and they marched along the bank of the Tigris. In the month of Simanu [March], they encamped against Nineveh. . . . For three months they subjected the city to a heavy siege. On the [?] day of the month Abu [May], they inflicted a major defeat upon [the Assyrians]. They [the besiegers] carried off the vast booty of the city and the temple and turned the city into a ruin heap.[58]

Most of the Assyrian records take the form of carved scenes and inscriptions on the walls of palaces and temples and show the major actions of the Assyrian

A Biblical Historical Account

The Bible contains several passages dealing with military campaigns of Babylonian and Assyrian kings. These include descriptions of the sieges of a number of Palestinian cities, the deportation of many Hebrews to Babylonia, and the fall of Assyria at the hands of the Medes and Babylonians. This example from the second book of Chronicles mentions the Assyrian king Sennacherib's military campaign against the Hebrew kingdom of Judah.

Sennacherib, king of Assyria, who was besieging Lachish [south of Jerusalem] with all his forces, sent his servants to Jerusalem to Hezekiah, king of Judah, and to all the people of Judah [saying], "On what are you relying, that you stand siege in Jerusalem. [Do] you not know what I and my fathers have done to all the peoples of other lands?"

2 Chronicles 32:10–13.

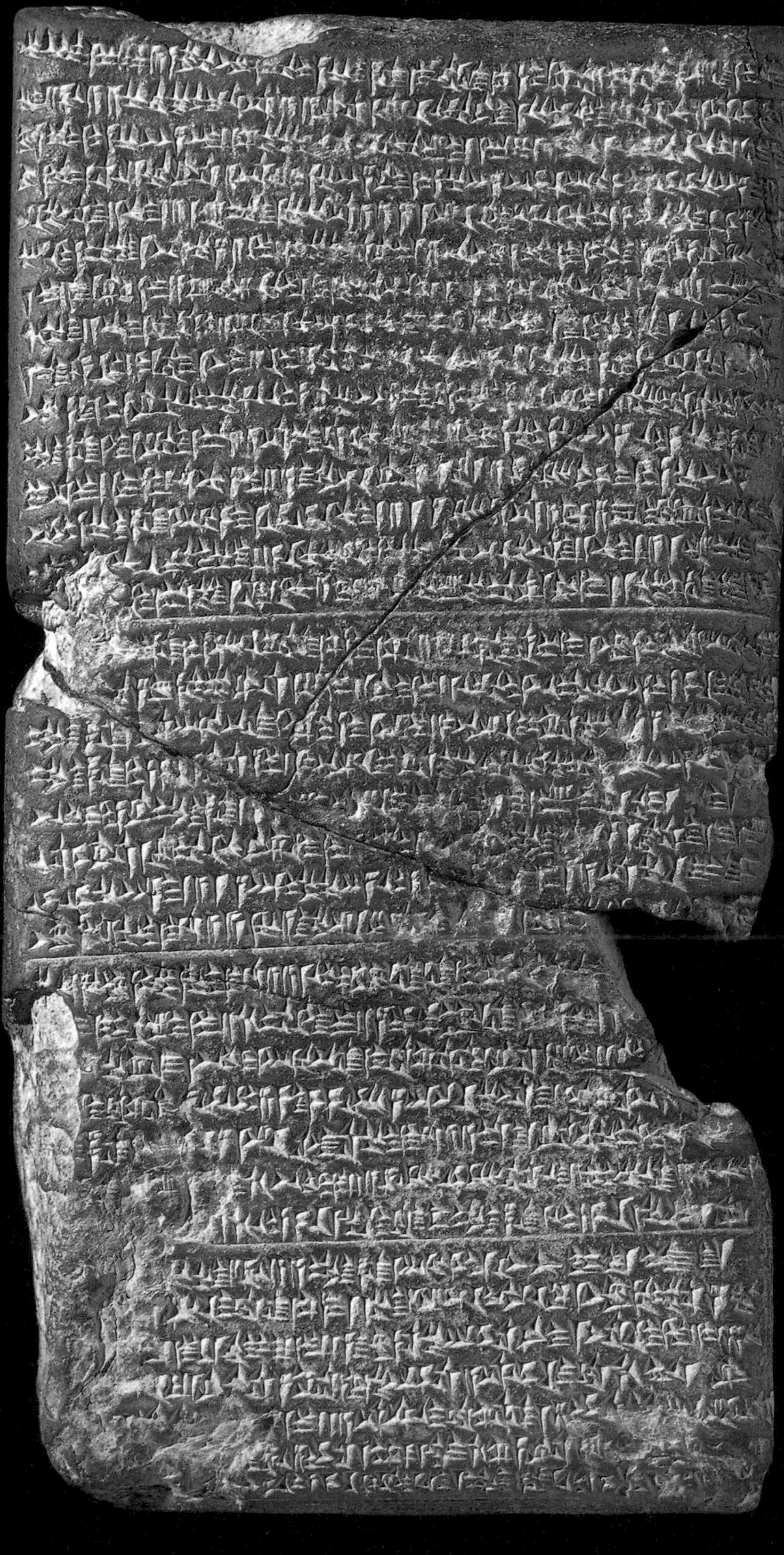

A tablet containing the Fall of Nineveh Chronicle, *one of a series of historical writings known collectively as the* Babylonian Chronicles, *which summarize the events of each year from 747–280* B.C.

kings. These were not fair accounts of people and events like those in modern history texts. The ancient records were created to glorify Assyria's kings and are therefore full of exaggerations and invented incidents; also, they make no mention of defeats, setbacks, or scandals. The deeds of some of the Assyrian and Babylonian kings are also mentioned in various books of the Hebrew Old Testament, some of which was written in Mesopotamia.

Eventually, a Babylonian priest named Berossus, who lived in the third century B.C., attempted to write a conventional, largely unbiased history of Mesopotamia. He sought to educate the Greeks, who then ruled Mesopotamia, about the civilizations that had come before in the area. Unfortunately, this work, the *Babylonaica*, survives only in pieces.

Some Greeks who either lived in or visited Mesopotamia also produced accounts dealing with the region's history and cultures. Important among these is the *Histories* by Herodotus, who lived in the fifth century B.C. Among other things, he described Babylon's famous defensive walls:

> [Babylon] is surrounded by a broad deep moat full of water, and within the moat there is a wall fifty cubits wide and two hundred high. [A cubit measured about 20 inches.] . . . On the top of the wall they constructed, along each edge, a row of one-roomed buildings facing inwards with enough space between for a four-horse chariot to pass. There are a hundred gates in the circuit of the wall, all of bronze.[59]

In writing the first known history text in the modern sense, Herodotus was guided by and brought together many of the scattered historical sources he found in the Near East. (He also conducted extensive interviews with residents of the area.) Many of those sources are now lost. So from a modern viewpoint, he and other Greek writers helped to fill some of the gaps in the incomplete but priceless and intriguing collection of surviving Mesopotamian literature.

Notes

Introduction: Tiny Remains of Vast Cultural Wealth

1. Stephen Bertman, *Handbook to Life in Ancient Mesopotamia*. New York: Facts On File, 2003, p. x.
2. Seton Lloyd, *The Art of the Ancient Near East*. London: Thames and Hudson, 1965, p. 9.
3. Wolfram von Soden, *The Ancient Orient*, trans. Donald G. Schley. Grand Rapids, MI: Eerdmans, 1994, p. 12.
4. H.W.F. Saggs, *Civilization Before Greece and Rome*. New Haven, CT: Yale University Press, 1991, p. 9.

Chapter One: Crafts and Craft Workers

5. Von Soden, *The Ancient Orient*, pp. 104–5.
6. Quoted in Washington State University, "The Code of Hammurabi." www.wsu.edu/~dee/MESO/CODE.HTM.
7. Bertman, *Handbook to Life in Ancient Mesopotamia*, p. 223.
8. Saggs, *Civilization Before Greece and Rome*, p. 196.
9. Gwendolyn Leick, *Historical Dictionary of Mesopotamia*. Lanham, MD: Scarecrow, 2003, p. 25.

10. Samuel N. Kramer, *Cradle of Civilization*. New York: Time-Life, 1978, p. 146.
11. Karen R. Nemet-Nejat, *Daily Life in Ancient Mesopotamia*. Peabody, MA: Hendrickson, 1998, pp. 297–99.
12. Bertman, *Handbook to Life in Ancient Mesopotamia*, pp. 229–30.

Chapter Two: Sculpture and Other Fine Arts

13. A. Leo Oppenheim, *Ancient Mesopotamia: Portrait of a Dead Civilization*. Chicago: University of Chicago Press, 1977, p. 329.
14. Chester G. Starr, *A History of the Ancient World*. New York: Oxford University Press, 1991, p. 135.
15. Bertman, *Handbook to Life in Ancient Mesopotamia*, p. 223.
16. Lloyd, *The Art of the Ancient Near East*, pp. 85–86.
17. Leick, *Historical Dictionary of Mesopotamia*, p. 33.
18. Norman B. Hunt, *Historical Atlas of Ancient Mesopotamia*. New York: Facts On File, 2004, p. 159.

Chapter Three: Language and Writing

19. Kramer, *Cradle of Civilization*, p. 11.

20. Saggs, *Civilization Before Greece and Rome*, p. 18.
21. Starr, *A History of the Ancient World*, p. 35.
22. Kramer, *Cradle of Civilization*, p. 121.
23. Saggs, *Civilization Before Greece and Rome*, p. 7.
24. Kramer, *Cradle of Civilization*, p. 127.
25. Quoted in Washington State University, "The Code of Hammurabi."
26. Quoted in Daniel D. Luckenbill, ed., *Ancient Records of Assyria and Babylonia*, vol. 1. New York: Greenwood, 1989, p. 40.
27. Quoted in Ancient Egypt Online, "The Amarna Letters; EA7, EA8 and EA9." www.ancientegyptonline.co.uk/EA7.html.
28. H.W.F. Saggs, *Babylonians*. Berkeley and Los Angeles: University of California Press, 2000, pp. 141–42.

Chapter Four: Scribes and Education

29. Gwendolyn Leick, *Mesopotamia: The Invention of the City*. New York: Penguin, 2001, p. 160.
30. Quoted in Nemet-Nejat, *Daily Life in Ancient Mesopotamia*, p. 62.
31. Quoted in Leick, *Mesopotamia*, p. 241.
32. Nemet-Nejat, *Daily Life in Ancient Mesopotamia*, p. 56.
33. Quoted in Electronic Text Corpus of Sumerian Literature, "Advice of a Supervisor to a Younger Scribe." http://etcsl.orinst.ox.ac.uk/cgi-bin/etcsl.cgi?text=t.5.1.3#.

34. Quoted in Kramer, *Cradle of Civilization*, p. 238.
35. Quoted in Leick, *Mesopotamia*, p. 162.
36. Quoted in Saggs, *Civilization Before Greece and Rome*, p. 107.
37. Pliny the Elder, *Natural History: A Selection,* trans. John H. Healy. New York: Penguin, 1991, p. 77.

Chapter Five: Epic Poetry

38. Nemet-Nejat, *Daily Life in Ancient Mesopotamia*, p. 65.
39. Bertman, *Handbook to Life in Ancient Mesopotamia*, p. 149.
40. Nemet-Nejat, *Daily Life in Ancient Mesopotamia*, p. 64.
41. Quoted in MythHome, "The Tablets Telling the Epic of Gilgamesh, Tablet 2, Enkidu and Gilgamesh Meet." www.mythome.org/gilgamesh2.html.
42. Quoted in MythHome, "The Tablets Telling the Epic of Gilgamesh, Tablet 8, Gilgamesh Laments, Fears Death, Says Good-bye to Enkidu." www.mythome.org/gilgamesh8.html.
43. Quoted in MythHome, "The Tablets Telling the Epic of Gilgamesh, Tablet 9, Gilgamesh Seeks Immortality and Meets a Scorpion." www.mythome.org/gilgamesh9.html.
44. Quoted in Christian Resource Institute, "*Enuma Elish:* 'When on High . . .'" www.cresourcei.org/enumaelish.html.
45. Enrico Ascalone, *Mesopotamia*, trans. Rosanna M. Giammanco Frongia.

Berkeley and Los Angeles: University of California Press, 2007, p. 96.

Chapter Six: Sacred and Secular Literature

46. Nemet-Nejat, *Daily Life in Ancient Mesopotamia*, pp. 62–63.
47. Bertman, *Handbook to Life in Ancient Mesopotamia*, p. 172.
48. Quoted in Jean Bottero, *Everyday Life in Ancient Mesopotamia*. Baltimore: Johns Hopkins University Press, 2001, p. 209.
49. Quoted in Kramer, *Cradle of Civilization*, p. 127.
50. Quoted in Kramer, *Cradle of Civilization*, p. 127.
51. Quoted in Kramer, *Cradle of Civilization*, p. 127.
52. Quoted in Electronic Text Corpus of Sumerian Literature, "Proverbs, Collection 3." http://etcsl.orinst.ox. ac.uk/cgi-bin/etcsl.cgi?text=t.6.1.0 &charenc=j#.
53. Quoted in Electronic Text Corpus of Sumerian Literature, "Proverbs, Collection 5." http://etcsl.orinst.ox.ac. uk/cgi-bin/etcsl.cgi?text=t.6.1.05& charenc=j#.
54. Quoted in Thorkild Jacobson, *The Treasures of Darkness: A History of Mesopotamian Religion*. New Haven, CT: Yale University Press, 1978, pp. 87–89.
55. Lamentations 2:7, 18.
56. Quoted in Electronic Text Corpus of Sumerian Literature, "Letter from Inanaka to the Goddess Nintinuga." http://etcsl.orinst.ox.ac.uk/cgi-bin/ etcsl.cgi?text=t.3.3.10&charenc=j#.
57. Quoted in A. Leo Oppenheim, ed., *Letters from Mesopotamia: Official, Business, and Private Letters on Clay Tablets from Two Millennia*. Chicago: University of Chicago Press, 1967, p. 85.
58. Quoted in Livius, "Fall of Nineveh Chronicle." www.livius.org/ne-nn/ nineveh/nineveh02.html.
59. Herodotus, *The Histories*, trans. Aubrey de Sélincourt. New York: Penguin, 1996, p. 113.

Glossary

amulet: An object thought to have magical and protective powers.

archive: A large collection of books or other written records.

bronze: An alloy, or mixture, of the metals copper and tin.

colophon: An identifying mark made by a scribe on a clay tablet or other writing surface.

cuneiform: An ancient Mesopotamian writing system that employed small wedge-shaped signs and symbols.

cylinder seal: A small, curved piece of stone (or other material) on which people etched images or words.

dubsar: A scribe.

dynasty: A family line of rulers.

edubba: "Tablet house"; a scribal school.

epic poem: A long literary work most often dealing with weighty themes, such as life and death, love and hate, and war and peace.

fresco: A painting done on wet plaster.

guild: A group of individuals who shared certain skills and lifestyles, most often members of a particular craft.

lamassi: "Bull-men"; large statues of human-headed bulls placed at the entrances to ancient Assyrian palaces.

lament (or lamentation): A sad poem or song bemoaning the death of a person or fall of a city.

loan words: Words that one language borrows from another.

lyre: A small harp.

malachite: A green material that forms when copper weathers.

ostraca: Broken pieces of pottery used as writing surfaces.

pantheon: A group of gods worshipped by a people or nation.

papyrus: A kind of paper made from a marsh plant.

proverb: A short, wise, and/or humorous saying passed from one generation to another.

psalms: Sacred hymns or songs.

relief (or bas-relief): A carved scene raised somewhat from a flat surface.

sage: A wise person, usually advanced in age.

scribe: In the ancient world, a person who used his or her reading and writing skills in some professional capacity.

stelae: Upright stone or metal slabs or markers bearing images, words, or both.

ummia: A specialist, usually an artisan or craft worker; the term *ummia* also denoted the headmaster of a scribal school.

Time Line

B.C.

ca. 9000
Agriculture begins in the Fertile Crescent, the area lying along the northern rim of the Mesopotamian plains.

ca. 4000
A slow-turning potter's wheel comes into use in Mesopotamia.

ca. 3300–3000
The Sumerians begin building the world's first cities.

ca. 3000
Bronze begins to be used in large quantities in Mesopotamia.

ca. 2141–2122
Reign of Gudea, king of Lagash, whose sculptors carve almost thirty statues of him.

ca. 2000
A faster-turning potter's wheel appears in Mesopotamia; an unknown Babylonian scribe writes a version of the famous epic poem about the early Mesopotamian hero Gilgamesh.

ca. 1813–1781
Reign of the early Assyrian king Shamshi-Adad, whose letters to and from his sons have survived.

ca. 1792–1750
Reign of Hammurabi, king of Babylonia, who issues the most comprehensive law code yet seen.

ca. 1600
The earliest surviving glass products are made in Mesopotamia.

ca. 1244–1208
Reign of Assyrian king Tukulti-Ninurta I, subject of the only surviving Assyrian epic poem.

ca. 1200
Iron smelting begins in Mesopotamia.

ca. 668–627
Reign of the Assyrian king Ashurbanipal, who is trained as a scribe and greatly expands the royal library.

334
The Macedonian Greek king Alexander the Great begins his swift conquest of the Persian Empire.

A.D.
634–651
Muslim Arab armies conquer much of Mesopotamia and other parts of the Near East.

1788
Danish-German scholar Karsten Niebuhr publishes ancient inscriptions

found in the ruins of the ancient city of Persepolis.

1849
Archaeologist Austen Henry Layard finds King Ashurbanipal's library at Nineveh.

1876
English scholar George Smith translates the ancient Babylonian epic poem *The Epic of Creation*.

1927
British archaeologist Charles Leonard Woolley discovers the Royal Standard of Ur, a magnificent mosaic dating from the third millennium B.C.

For More Information

Books

Stephen Bertman, *Handbook to Life in Ancient Mesopotamia*. New York: Facts On File, 2003. A fact-filled, easy-to-read guide to the region's peoples, leaders, religious beliefs and myths, social customs, languages, arts and crafts, and much more.

J.A. Black, *Reading Sumerian Poetry*. Ithaca: Cornell University Press, 1998. An excellent introduction to Sumerian poetry, with several new translations by the author.

Jeremy Black et al., eds., *The Literature of Ancient Sumer*. New York: Oxford University Press, 2006. A comprehensive and useful collection of Sumerian literature of all types.

Dominique Collon, *Ancient Near Eastern Art*. Berkeley and Los Angeles: University of California Press, 1995. A very well written overview of the subject.

Giovanni Curatola et al., *The Art and Architecture of Mesopotamia*. New York: Abbeville, 2007. A well-illustrated volume that covers all the major examples of ancient Sumerian, Babylonian, and Assyrian art.

Benjamin R. Foster, ed., *From Distant Days: Myths, Tales, and Poetry of Ancient Mesopotamia*. Bethesda, MD: CDL, 1995. A very readable collection of translations of ancient Mesopotamian literature.

Norman B. Hunt, *Historical Atlas of Ancient Mesopotamia*. New York: Facts On File, 2004. Contains dozens of excellent maps helpful to those interested in ancient Mesopotamia.

Maureen G. Kovacs, trans., *The Epic of Gilgamesh*. Palo Alto, CA: Stanford University Press, 1990. One of the better recent translations of the most famous epic poem produced in ancient Mesopotamia.

Gwendolyn Leick, *Mesopotamia: The Invention of the City*. New York: Penguin, 2001. In her detailed examination of key Mesopotamian cities, Leick, one of the foremost authorities on ancient Mesopotamia, discusses numerous aspects of the region's art, education, and literature.

A. Leo Oppenheim et al., *Glass and Glassmaking in Ancient Mesopotamia*. Cranbury, NJ: Associated University Presses, 1988. A detailed look at this important ancient Mesopotamian craft.

Michael Roaf, *Cultural Atlas of Mesopotamia and the Ancient Near East*. New York: Facts On File, 1990. This well-illustrated book provides a useful synopsis of the main cultural aspects of the ancient Mesopotamian peoples.

Web Sites

Ancient Mesopotamia: Archaeology, The Oriental Institute of the University of Chicago (http://oi.uchicago.edu/OI/MUS/ED/TRC/MESO/archaeology.html). This site features several links to brief but excellent articles about ancient Mesopotamia.

The Behistun Inscription, Livius (www.livius.org/be-bm/behistun/behistun01.html). An overview of the famous Persian rock carving, with links to related topics.

About Cuneiform Writing, University of Pennsylvania Museum of Archaeology and Anthropology (www.upenn.edu/museum/Games/cuneiform.html). An excellent introduction to the ancient Mesopotamian art of cuneiform writing.

The Epic of Atrahasis, Livius (www.livius.org/as-at/atrahasis/atrahasis.html). Contains a translation of the surviving parts of this ancient Mesopotamian epic, which mentions the same great flood described in the Bible.

Hammurabi, Humanistic Texts (www.humanistictexts.org/hammurabi.htm). Contains excellent translations of many of the famous Babylonian ruler's laws.

Lamassu, Livius (www.livius.org/la-ld/lamassu/lamassu.html). A brief but useful description of the giant, human-headed bull statues that guarded the entrances to Assyrian palaces.

Index

Picture Credits

Cover: Image copyright John Said, 2008. Used under license from Shutterstock.com

Alinari/Art Resource, NY, 31

AP Images, 27, 41

The Art Archive/Archaeological Museum Baghdad/Gianni Dagli Orti, 66

The Art Archive/Musée du Louvre Paris/Gianni Dagli Orti, 54

The Art Archive/Private Collection/ Eileen Tweedy, 76

Art Resource, NY, 26

Bildarchiv Preussischer Kulturbesitz/ Art Resource, NY, 67, 72

The Bridgeman Art Library/Getty Images, 52

© British Museum/Art Resource, NY, 20, 22, 28, 30, 34, 69, 71

Roger Fenton/George Eastman House/ Hulton Archive/Getty Images, 45

Werner Forman/Art Resource, NY, 19, 60

Gale, Cengage Learning, 9

Giraudon/Art Resource, NY, 32

Erich Lessing/Art Resource, NY, 15, 23, 36, 49, 57, 79, 82, 84

Image copyright © The Metropolitan Museum of Art/Art Resource, NY, 21

Réunion des Musées Nationaux/Art Resource, NY, 17, 42, 47, 64

Karim Sahib/AFP/Getty Images, 10

Steve Zmina, 40

About the Author

Historian and award-winning writer Don Nardo has published many books about the ancient world, including *Life in Ancient Athens; The Etruscans; Life of a Roman Gladiator; Religion in Ancient Egypt;* literary companions to the works of Homer, Sophocles, and Euripides; histories of the Assyrian and Persian empires; and Greenhaven Press's encyclopedias of ancient Greece, ancient Rome, and Greek and Roman mythology. He lives with his wife, Christine, in Massachusetts.